REPRODUCING CLASS

REPRODUCING CLASS

Education, Neoliberalism, and the
Rise of the New Middle Class in Istanbul

Henry J. Rutz and Erol M. Balkan

Berghahn Books
New York • Oxford

First published in 2009 by

Berghahn Books
www.berghahnbooks.com

©2009, 2010 Henry J. Rutz and Erol M. Balkan
First paperback edition published in 2010

Library of Congress Cataloging-in-Publication Data

Rutz, Henry J.
Reproducing class : education, neoliberalism, and the rise of the new middle
   class in Istanbul / Henry J. Rutz and Erol M. Balkan.—1st ed.
      p. cm.
   Includes bibliographical references and index.
   ISBN 978-1-84545-562-0 (hbk) — 978-1-84545-780-8 (pbk)
   1. Middle class—Turkey—History—20th century.   I. Balkan, Erol M. II. Title.
HT684.R88 2009
305.5'50949618—dc22   2008047820

British Library Cataloguing in Publication Data
A catalogue record for this book is available from the British Library

Printed in the United States on acid-free paper

ISBN: 978-1-84545-562-0 Hardback, 978-1-84545-780-8 Paperback

For Doris
For Neşecan, Osman, and Mehmet

Contents

PREFACE

One of the most salient social phenomena of our times is the rise of global cities and the associated remaking of national middle classes into global new middle classes as a consequence of economic globalization through global corporations that are restructuring welfare states and making them into neoliberal states. Much has already been written about economic differentiation within the middle class as a result of deregulation of national markets and the unprecedented changes taking place in work and family life. Less well documented but equally salient for class formation is the effect of global processes on the changing culture of the urban middle class. And one of the most salient aspects of middle class social reproduction, old or new, is quality education as a path to occupation destinations and a cultural ideology of consumption that reinvents what it means to live "a comfortable life." This urban ethnography of middle class formation through selective education is a contribution to the larger project of the comparative study of elite education and formation of middle classes in this era of globalization. It comes at a time when the value of testing in the context of human capital development and the increasing option of privatized alternatives to public education are being aired in newspapers and on television and when families are seeking alternative forms of schooling for their children.

While the relationship between the new middle class and selective education in world cities is everywhere becoming more apparent, the dynamics of class formation by means of selective education remain particular to state formation, national economic policies, family formation, local cultures, and national education systems.[1] This book is an ethnographic account of those dynamics as expressed in the struggle of middle-class families in Istanbul to provide their children with quality education during a period of transition during an early phase of global integration. Its internal logic turns on families' perception that for their eleven-year-old children to have a comfortable life, they must win the national state-directed Selective Middle Schools Examinations (SMSEs). The odds that they will fail are daunting and at times overwhelming. The result is a social drama in which wives act against their own will and become exam-obsessed mothers who engineer and design their children as test machines, while fathers, embittered by what they perceive to be a corrupt system that would turn families into an instrument of state policy and expose them to the economic exploitation of a market for education services, go into deep denial or passive resistance.

This story is told in part through the voices of parents who provided us with discourse themes from their narrative accounts of the system and their struggle, itself a complex construction that requires a reflexive stance on bureaucratic rationality and standardization. These interpretive themes appear in different chapters and become part of the larger analysis of a changing middle class from 1983 to 1997. From one perspective, middle-class formation is shaped by a transformation in state formation and market forces that have bifurcated and transformed what it means to be middle class. From a perspective inside the middle class, families became liberalized and made the agency of their own class reproduction, including a class awareness of what is at stake. We emphasize that not only is the Istanbul new middle class conscious of its structural location in economy and society but its families are able to articulate their interests. This study explores the meaning of belonging to the Istanbul middle class through their discourse on education, testing, and their own analysis of the whole system that we will refer to as the *field of competition relations*. Both state and families view their relationship to each other in terms of objective conditions of existence for the reproduction of a privileged class in Turkish society.

The historical moment of transition in Turkey that marks the temporal phase of this social drama is known in official discourse as the *liberalization episode*. It began with an economic crisis in the 1970s that led to a coup in 1980. The Turkish economy did an about-face by turning away from protectionist state policies of import substitution to deregulated export-oriented policies that opened Turkey in general, and Istanbul in particular, to flows of global capital, information technology, telecommunications, and trade goods. In the Turkish case, the economic transition was from state policies of import substitution that protected national industries and agriculture to state policies that deregulated finance capital and imposed new burdens of taxation on the middle class. Economic restructuring that resulted in a bifurcation within the middle class exacerbated an already widening gap between the rich and the poor, which contributed to persistent economic crisis and posed a threat to political and societal stability.

We chose Istanbul as the site of this study for two reasons, one having to do with Istanbul itself, the other having to do with method. The first is that globalizing cities in every country are the best place to observe the dynamics of middle-class formation in the context of globalization processes. It is in globalizing cities like Istanbul that competition for access to the best education plays a pivotal role in middle-class transformation over the last several decades. The economic and cultural risks and opportunities associated with middle-class capital accumulation were greatest there, and the disparities in class competition most apparent and observable. Their greatest impact was felt in Istanbul, which had always been a world city and a center of commerce and long-distance trade across imperial and, in the twentieth century to the present, national borders.

The city also had long been a center of education. In Istanbul today, there is an unambiguously close relationship between selective education and the formation of a small, privileged Turkish upper middle class. Issues of cosmopolitan culture are part of the larger picture, but they also become directly relevant when we look at selective education. In Turkey, not unlike much of Europe, there is an aristocracy of intellectuals that is inscribed in the line of demarcation between the education of the upper middle class and other classes or class fragments. Foreign language and culture are among the distinctive markers of an upper middle class. Distinctive subcultures of the upper middle class have developed around school ties and networks of classmates. And selective middle schools, not coincidentally, instruct in foreign language. Most of the best middle schools are in Istanbul, some of its most prestigious universities are there, and most of its private schools and all of the new private universities built in the 1990s are there. Migrants who are already middle class or are middle-class aspirants view education as one of the main factors for family migration to Istanbul as well as to Ankara or Izmir. The rapid growth of state investment in selective Anadolu schools, accompanied by a turn toward a neoliberal policy of the expansion in private schools at all levels of the education hierarchy after decades of state resistance, are signature education policies of the liberalization episode. From 1983 to 1997, the key point of entry to class privilege that flows from access to the best schools was entry to middle school. In Turkey, access to the best middle schools is attained through the national Selective Middle Schools Examinations (SMSEs), state-controlled and managed tests that began in 1983.

When in 1983 the Ministry of National Education introduced the SMSEs, Istanbul's middle-class families had the most to gain but also the most to lose from a new national selection system that was labeled "objective" and "fair." The annual national examinations quickly became an arena for intensive middle-class competition among families, which planned for the examinations and prepared to win places in schools that offered the highest probability of a child entering a small number of elite universities in Turkey or, even more desirable for many new middle class families, scholarships in universities abroad.

The second reason for the choice of a particular site for the study of middle-class formation has to do with our approach to class analysis through field methods of research that become the basis of an ethnographic tradition of writing. In our case, an economist and an anthropologist offer the prospect of integrating global, national, and local perspectives on the relationship between economy and culture in a balanced analysis of different kinds of data and information, from the statistical and analytical perspective of macroeconomics to the participant observer and interview approach of interpretive cultural anthropology. In the ethnography, this collaborative effort appears as a commitment to give the state and market their due as agencies of class formation while acknowledging the importance of family practices as the key agent of class reproduction and social consciousness. The overall movement that reflects the structure and organization of the book is from global through national to local frameworks of analysis, but we do not tell the story in a rigid, linear progression. Subjects of different chapters require different durations of time and locations of place that reflect uneven development, contingent history, and variable rates of change in different institutions. The organization and content of the entire book reflect our attempt to achieve these methodological aims and, in the final analysis, contribute to a comparative understanding of the emergence of new middle classes around the globe.

Notes

1. For recent scholarship on issues in educational development and social transformation in a global economy, see the essays in Mebrahtu, Crossley and Johnson 2000. Jacque Hallak, in his essay on "Globalization and Its Impact on Education," emphasizes the impact on global acceleration in economic freedom, technological innovation (especially in communications), and interdependence among these fields of innovation (2000: 21–40).

Acknowledgements

During a decade of collaboration, this project has accumulated its debts to organizations and persons. For financial support, Rutz is indebted to the Fulbright Foundation for a Senior Lecturer award that allowed him to teach at Boğaziçi University during the academic year 1991–92. Funds from the William R. Kenan Chair at Hamilton College funded aspects of fieldwork from 1990 to 1994, including intensive Turkish language study at Boğaziçi University. Hamilton College Faculty Travel and Support grants funded field research in the summers of 1991, 1993, and 1995. Hamilton College granted sabbaticals during fall 1990 for the purpose of reconnaissance and spring 1997 for final field research. Balkan is indebted to Hamilton College for its support for the survey and interviews conducted in Istanbul during 1993–97 and again in 2006. We acknowledge the generous support of the Wenner-Gren Foundation for Anthropological Research for a senior grant that contributed to the completion in 1993 of the Istanbul Socioeconomic Household Survey. The Cultural Anthropology Program of the National Science Foundation Award No. 9506123 supported interviews of Istanbul families from January to June 1997.

Turkish colleagues, friends, and families provided the social and emotional support that is so necessary to the morale and success of any project involving fieldwork and ethnography. Ahmet Tonak introduced Rutz to Ayşe Öncü, the chair of the Sociology Department, who was instrumental in making it possible for Rutz to assume a Fulbright Fellowship at Boğaziçi University. Ayşe was unstinting in her support of Rutz during his stay and she, along with Nükhet Sirman, Belgin Tekçe, Fred Shorter, Ferhunde Özbay, Leyla Neyzi, and Peter Taylor were generous in their hospitality, their collegial counsel and advice, and their sharing of friends and family. Parts of this book germinated in conversations over dinner or while relaxing in their homes. Fulbright Senior Research Fellow Daniel Bates and his wife Judith, Roger Samuel and Virginia Johnston, Istanbul Director of American Research Institute in Turkey Tony Greenwood and Gülen Aptas, Orhan and Pamela Saroz, and the whole Çakmak family and kinswoman Nergis

Çakıroğlu offered their hospitality and friendship. Rutz is especially grateful to his Turkish language teacher Sabahat Sansa, who persevered in the classroom while teaching him much about Turkish culture. Balkan is grateful to Sungur Savran for his support and thoughtful comments. Rutz is grateful to Bonnie Urciuoli for many stimulating conversations that have influenced the argument of the book. Robin Vanderwall formatted this book and stimulated further conversation about its content.

Taped interviews and the Istanbul Socioeconomic Household Survey were a main part of our early research design. We would be remiss if we did not acknowledge a major contribution of the following parents, educators, teachers, tutors, and school owners who submitted to taped interviews: Hürriyet and Levent Konyar; Yasemin and Babür Bayındır; Fügen, Elif, and Tuncay Pulcu; Feray and Zeynep Öz; Birkan Yetkin; Şule Sevin; Sevil Tuğrul; Dicle Öldürülenoğlu; Lale Ünal; Güler Esmergil; Mehmet Ali Neyzi; Ergüder Pasin; Füsun Kuzuoğlu; Vitale Meşulam; Belma Ikiz; Sinan Cağdas; Şükran Başkurt; Temel and Ayşe Gültepe; Ahmet Dura; Abbas Güçlü; Tomris and Hudai Gasemaz; Nuray and Erol Turan; Serap, Kasım, and Özge Taşar; Jale and Sedat Evener; Meral Alpay; Nurten Arakon; Dündar Uçar; Yeşim Inanır; Dilek and Aydın Yardım; and Inci and Deniz Kayabay. The collection of data for the Istanbul Socioeconomic Household Survey was accomplished by using the instrument of a survey questionnaire to interview 550 households. We acknowledge the contribution of the following research assistants who were recruited to locate informants and administer the questionnaire: Hikmet Kuşhan, Aslı Tuğrul, Hürriyet Konyar, Janet Çorlu, Gizem Kilislioğlu, and Kürşat Yaşar. We also thank another research assistant, Nafiz Akşehirlioğlu, for his diligent search into popular culture and lifestyle materials. Aslı Tuğrul, C. Gökçe Güldal, and Işık Ökte transcribed and translated the taped interviews. Baran Tekkora and Taylan Baykut helped Balkan format and put into computer form the raw data from the Istanbul Socioeconomic Household Survey.

We are grateful to Doris Rutz and Neşecan Balkan for improving the argument of this book by their thoughtful and careful editing of each chapter and also by their careful questioning that led to numerous redactions of the final manuscript. Without their continuous support, this project would not have been possible.

Introduction

It is a beautiful Saturday morning in late May. In Istanbul, spring is in the air; there is not the usual noise and scurrying around that one encounters during harried weekdays. It is the kind of morning when young parents are out and about with their children, when there is time to explore neighborhood surroundings without purpose or direction. We have been part of this scene countless times on our weekend walks around the backstreets of Beyoğlu (formerly Pera) and Karaköy (formerly Galata), two of the oldest areas of non-Turkish settlement that predate the establishment of Constantinople as the imperial city of the Byzantine empire. These districts housed guilds, foreign merchants, and dignitaries during the centuries of Ottoman rule that preceded the founding of the Turkish Republic in 1923. In the nineteenth century, Pera was the center of European modernist culture and continues to serve that function with its fin de siècle architecture, foreign consulates, churches, film theaters, restaurants, coffee houses, taverns, bookstores, galleries, and marketplaces. The main avenue, named Istiklal Caddesi (Independence Boulevard), is emblematic of the way in which Istanbul merges its Turkish national identity with its cosmopolitan identity influenced by European ideas about modernism. Ironically, the Turkish Republic emerged slowly after the First World War until Mustafa Kemal, later to be known as Atatürk (Father Turk), fought a successful war of independence against France, Britain, Italy, and Greece. In Taksim Square at the head of Independence Boulevard, there is an awe-inspiring and beautiful statue of Atatürk surrounded by his compatriots from every walk of life. Normally, the boulevard is a promenade for lovers, tourists, shoeshine boys, and other characters from all parts of the city who assemble to stroll and gaze at each other.

On this particular Saturday morning, the structure of feeling is different. The year is 1996, the date May 24, the time an hour away from eleven o'clock. We register these precise facts because we are walking briskly in the same direction as others, with purpose. Following a multitude of parents with their children in hand, we turn off Sıraselviler, one of the main streets in the district of Cihangir, and wind down Turnacı Başı Street to an elementary school that happens to be located next to the Greek Consulate. Others have already assembled. There is a look of nervousness on the faces of parents, an *unusual quietness in children, and stillness in the air. We sense a feeling of apprehension, yet also single-minded determination. A few parents greet each other before turning their gaze toward the pavement or the sky, or just staring at an empty middle distance. The children are from different elementary schools, but as fifth-graders they share the same intention. There are a few older people milling about, no doubt surrogate parents. Expressionless children stand dutifully by the side of a parent or ward, foregoing an opportunity to glance at each other.*

We share this structure of feeling because others like them have shared their hopes, dreams, and anxieties with us. We are there to observe, at one moment in one location, an annual event that occurs simultaneously in designated venues across the nation. We know that a large majority of the participants in this ritual are privileged children of a relatively small proportion of the Turkish population. Their families share a class resemblance, but retain many differences in their character and beliefs. Years of preparation have brought them together at the door of this school.

At precisely eleven o'clock, the heavy wooden door opens and a man steps out; without a word, he motions the children to enter. They move toward the door with a studied pace. At the door, he checks the name of each child against his list. A few parents venture a step through the doorway for one last hug, interrupted by a gesture that separates parent from child. After the last child enters, the man disappears behind the closing door. The sudden separation, we surmise, must be jarring, antithetic to the emotional closeness that develops between mother and child during their years of shared preparation and planning that have brought them to this school on this day. An hour and ten minutes will have passed before the door again opens. Inside, each child will have demonstrated the skills of speed and accuracy by answering one hundred multiple-choice questions. Outside, parents are thinking, "one chance only."

Most of the parents are mothers, and most are equipped with cell phones. They pace up and down the street but keep the door in sight, stop, sit for a moment on old stone walls across from the consulate, nervously occupying themselves by calling close relatives, neighbors, and friends who are awaiting word—any word. The calls are repeated frequently despite the absence of any news from inside the school. Cigarettes are lit and extinguished before they are spent. Once in a while, a car shows up. The driver, no doubt a husband or close relative, confers in low tones with the mother, then drives off. This act of disappearing and reappearing seems incongruous with the emotional tone of the event. The waiting seems unbearably long as mothers glance at their watches.

Suddenly, the door opens. Children come pouring out; some are wearing smiles, others subdued. None are exuberant. Parents rush to their child, embrace her or him, lift the child off her or his feet. They are delirious with joy and express enormous sighs of relief; sighs of adult exhaustion more from the mothers than the fathers. Abruptly, every child is whisked into a car or hurried up the street to attend a debriefing at home, where close friends, neighbors, and family members await to smother the child in loving security. No doubt there will be a reward. Mothers will thank their child for working with them—another incongruity, as if the child were working for his or her mother.

Relief gives way to heightened tension in the days that follow, as parents who chose to enter their child in this national test await news of the results. Within a week, the official results are published in national newspapers in the form of long lists of identification numbers of the children, together with their numerical score to the third decimal place.

The list is rank ordered, highest to lowest scores. The word is out—winners take all. Not even a second chance. Elimination. For weeks, on the front pages and in feature stories of national print media, winners reveal the names behind the numbers, and appellations of superiority are attached to them in newspapers that feature stories about "super" students that display the photos of winners, at times with their "super" tutors, sometimes their parents, but rarely with mothers, or with the elementary school teacher who taught the same child for five years. The private middle schools that are in competition with each other to select the best of the winners are themselves referred to by the press as "five-star" schools, closing the circle of symbolic capital.

Some of the most sought after middle schools in the country happen to be in the immediate vicinity of the event we observed. The oldest and most venerable school in the country is Galatasaray Lisesi (lycée), a few steps from the Greek Consulate onto Istiklal Boulevard. By a historical particularity, Galatasaray happens to be a special public school founded in the late Ottoman period as a school for training imperial pages as part of reforms referred to as Tanzimat. The school was reorganized in 1868 as a modern lycée (grades six to eleven, including middle school grades six to eight, and high school grades nine to eleven), influenced by France. Lessons were taught in both Turkish and French. A popular history of the area published in 1972 refers to the school as the "best as well as the most famous Turkish lycée." (Sumner-Boyd and Freely 1989: 104) Today it no longer is considered the "best" school by the state or most parents, but it continues to enjoy the reputation of being the most intellectual lycée, perhaps because of its commitment to a classical curriculum.

We stroll down Istiklal Boulevard from Galatasaray Lisesi to Alman Lisesi (German) and continue on past the museum and house of the venerable Whirling Dervishes, representative of a different genealogy and pedagogical heritage. Then down the hill past Galata Tower, the center of the medieval Genoese merchant community, to arrive at Avusturya Lisesi (Austrian, middle school). Continuing our stroll along the side of the hill in Galata, we circle back around to St. Benoit Lisesi (French). Had we continued farther along the hillside we would have arrived back at Taksim Circle, where Istiklal Boulevard begins. Nearby is Notre Dame de Sion Lisesi (French).

By international treaty, private foreign schools were protected and have survived over three generations to become the most sought-after schools in the country. Most are in Istanbul, all are private, all teach in both Turkish and foreign languages, and all have acquired a pedigree that precedes the founding of the Turkish Republic in 1923. To complete the Istanbul list, we include Saint Joseph Lisesi (French), Sankt George Avusturya Kız Lisesi (Austrian, for girls), Sankt George Avusturya Lisesi ve Ticaret Okulu (Austrian), Saint Michel Fransız Lisesi (French), İtalyan Lisesi (Italian), Üsküdar Amerikan Lisesi (American), and Robert Lisesi (American). In all, eleven private foreign elite schools that together have an enrollment of only several thousand seats.

For some decades now, Robert Lisesi has been, by acclamation of media and popular assent, the "best" high school in Turkey. Founded in 1863 by an American missionary and philanthropist, in its early years it became a university that for decades was called "the finest institution of higher learning in Turkey." In 1971, the original Robert College for men (the high school) moved from its hilltop site overlooking the narrows of the Bosphorus Strait and the village of Bebek to the campus of the American College for Girls. This girls' high school and the boys' high school were united and the institution became *the co-ed Robert College or Robert Lisesi. The campus is sited on a hillside surrounded by ample grasslands and trees, overlooking the Bosphorus Strait and the village of Arnavutköy on the shore road, a short distance from the center of the city.*

What secular rite of passage is being performed here? Ask anyone at the 24 May event and she or he will say that the test is not just any test. The official name of it is the Private Selective Middle Schools Examinations (*Özel Okullar Sınavı*) (hereafter, "SMSE"). The test is created, organized, managed, monitored, scored, and recorded by a test unit within the Ministry of National Education (*Milli Eğitim Bakanlığı*). Of all the ministries of the Turkish state, only the military bureaucracy has an equivalent standing. Education was viewed as the foundation of the republic and its modernizing aspirations.

Why are parents so anxious? A child can take the test only once, and that one time must be in fifth grade between the ages of eleven and twelve. Istanbul is a large, busy, and noisy metropolis. It would not be unusual to get caught in traffic, for a child to be sick that day, or for parents to have their own problems or obligations that required them to be elsewhere. If the child has an anxiety attack during the test, a need to relieve her- or himself, or any other conceivable act, there is no recourse. No second chance. To underscore this point, middle school graduates who choose to take the annual national University Entrance Examinations and fail may retake them numerous times.

What is the significance of this event to the families that participate in it? Winning this race (*yarış*) means more to them than anything else. When we ask why, they repeatedly offer the same comment that "education in Turkey has an absolute value." But why the test, when public schools and many private schools do not require it? Winning this race, they say, means the chance "to have a comfortable life." Parents, when pressed to clarify their gloss on our query, respond by saying that "we want our children to have the life we have, but in Turkey today it is more difficult."

Who participates and who does not? Its scope is nationwide, but only a small fraction of eligible families choose to enter the SMSEs. Nearly a million children were eligible in 1996, but only three hundred thousand students competed for less than five hundred Anadolu middle schools in 1996. About seventeen thousand children competed for several hundred private middle schools that together had only nine thousand seats to fill. The spatial distribution of elite schools is extreme. The difference between the two types of selective schools— public Anadolu and private schools—index a class difference between the families of the core middle class and the new middle class. Private schools are beyond the economic capital of core middle-class families, and private schools are clustered in a few urban centers where the neoliberal economy is visible on the landscape. The center of elite education is Istanbul, where demand is the greatest and the competition has become fierce.

By standards of Istanbul core middle-class earning power, tuition and costs of sending a child to a private school are exorbitant to the point of eliminating middle-class families from competing in the private SMSEs. Cost of education for families increased above inflation steadily during the 1980s and 1990s, at a time when new middle-class families were joining the ranks of the established Istanbul upper middle class.

Upper middle-class families of Istanbul and elsewhere in Turkey have sent their children to elite private foreign schools since the founding of the Turkish Republic in 1923. The new private schools that appeared after 1980 are a response to the appearance of new middle-class families and their aspirations. The emerging new middle class was on its way to achieving a collective interest in intergenerational accumulation and social reproduction by means of education that would reflect not only its education aspirations but also its claim to new economy jobs, class privilege in the eyes of the neoliberal state, and an emerging postmodern consumer lifestyle that transformed the appearance and space of an Istanbul metropolitan region.

The tale told at the beginning of this Introduction gets underneath structural issues that occupy the early chapters of the book and foregrounds subjectivities and sensibilities of the agents of class reproduction viewed through the lens of the selective middle schools examinations.

Prior to 1980, the Ministry of National Education was hostile toward private education of all sorts, which it viewed as an attack on the foundational principles of the republic and the role of education in creating a national culture by inculcating the duties of citizenship. The introduction of the test in 1983 was close enough to parents' memories of their own childhoods free from the demands that the state was now imposing on their children. They watched their neighbors and friends as the test became more competitive with each passing year and the annual cost of private education began to outpace inflation. Their anger went beyond the test per se to how preparation for the test affected the education of their children, a loss of childhood, and a disruption in their daily lives. Parents perceived the test negatively, as an instrument designed to eliminate all but a few. The tension between a belief in the necessity of the test and its violent intrusion in the lives of the family shaped their narratives of parenthood and childhood.[1]

The organization of the book addresses questions about the relation of education hierarchies to class hierarchies, the role that the neoliberal state and market together play in shaping class formation through education, and the agency of families in reproducing their own class privilege and values.

Remarkably, after 1980, especially during the decade of the 1990s and continuing into the present, there have been increases in private investment in schools at all levels of education, large enough that the government declared private education to be a new economic sector in national accounts. During this same period, Istanbul public education had reached a crisis of overcrowded classrooms, a shortage of teachers due in part to poor salaries, and a decline in quality (kalite) education. The public education crisis in Istanbul was partly due to population pressure after three decades of in-migration to cities from other provinces. Istanbul was the main destination of migrants from all provinces in Turkey. Other cities experienced in-migration primarily from provinces within their own region. The centripetal force of Istanbul in the context of class and education is made visible in an Istanbul population that has increased from one million in 1950 to ten million in 2000.

The global phenomenon we focus on in Istanbul is the appearance, over the past several decades, of new middle classes in globalizing cities around the world. These urban new middle classes, it is argued, are the social outcome of the policies and practices of states that have embraced a cultural ideology of neoliberalism and an economy of neoliberal markets. The result is an increase in the complexity and growth of new markets that have generated capital growth of all kinds—material, social, and symbolic-cultural. In the history of accumulation, we live at a time when the current scope, size, and rate of accumulation has restructured the relation between state and citizen, one social class and another, and raised questions about access and equity. The education of new middle classes in many countries is viewed by neoliberal states as human capital that has a price in the market and contributes to growth in the new economy.[2]

This book is an exploration of the question, how does the Turkish neoliberal state shape its economy and culture to form a new middle class, and how does that class reproduce itself? By default, we indirectly address the decline of an industrial core middle class. Ours is an ethnographic case study that focuses on Istanbul, Turkey's globalizing city.[3] We argue that fields of competitive relations, primarily in education and property, but also lifestyle, are among the most important fields to interrogate.

In Turkey, the neoliberal state and market are institutionalized sources of agency that realize the (neoliberal) new middle class as an emerging global middle class. The Istanbul new middle class, we argue, is the expression and result of the neoliberal state's elevation of the private market over other institutions that were deemed important during the previous era of building a nation through the instruments of a welfare state economy based on state enterprises. We refer to the middle class of this era as the *industrial core middle class*. The neoliberal state, we argue, through the exercise of its hegemony over social spaces, class privileges, and access to quality education, creates the conditions for and is the instrument by which access and equity are regulated and controlled in this era of the accumulation of capital on a global scale. Within this framework of neoliberal state and market, we explore the agency of the family as the main institution of new middle class reproduction.

Urban Ethnography and the Ethnographic Object

How were changes in middle-class formation during the liberalization episode affected by globalizing processes, and how were these refracted in the changing cityscape of Istanbul? This question has embedded in it another prior question about how the middle class is constituted as an object of study. Before we had determined the exact subject, namely, education practices of families and households that are central to the question of how a middle class is reproduced and transformed, we had intuitions and made self-evident observations about what constituted a middle class. These were based on our knowledge from several sources, including the literature on social class and our many conversations with people in Istanbul about the salience of our concept of class for exploring the relationship between education and social hierarchies. To these sources were added intuitions and experience from living in the city as well as more formal and recorded observations and interviews.

In one sense, fieldwork in Istanbul began for one of us in childhood. Balkan, who was born and grew up in a middle-class household in Bakırköy, now the largest and most populous district of Istanbul, went to Kadıköy Maarif Koleji, renamed Kadıköy Anadolu Lisesi when the state created the first five Anadolu middle schools in the 1950s in an attempt to meet middle-class families demand for quality education.

During the academic year of 1991–92, Rutz taught at Boğaziçi University. He taught a course in fieldwork methods that resulted in fifty-five case studies detailing economic, social, and cultural relations and functions of Istanbul kinship and household formation. With high agreement, students were able to use the names of city districts as a proxy to locate the social space of a middle class.

Methodology

Decisions about this book's problematic, methodology, and scope frame decisions such as what methods to deploy for gathering the necessary kinds of information from which to make interpretations and upon which to base conclusions. On the most general level, the book is about the multiple agencies of the neoliberal state, market, and family in making new middle classes in this era of globalization.

Ethnography is understood to include interpretations and conclusions based on extended periods of observation and interview. Ethnographers embrace both objectivities and subjectivities as information to be interpreted through their own methodology that nevertheless is recorded and transformed by our interpretation of their interpretations of themselves. Social and cultural knowledge remain incomplete, at times ambiguous, and open to scrutiny.

An apposite metaphor for our approach to methods is illustrated by Pablo Picasso's painting entitled *The Studio* (1927–28).[4] To the viewer, the painting exists through the image of multiple planes on a two-dimensional canvas, each with different colors, hues, and textures, which together create meaning for the artist. His subject is the object of his gaze, but the observer also interprets what is painted on the canvas. In *The Studio*, the painter has placed himself in the painting, discernible as an outline of his figure, looking at his subject, who also is figured in outline in another plane on the canvas. The observer sees different planes signified by different colors in the space between the artist and his subject. The viewer discerns table-like, vase-like, framed picture-like planes that together suggest the context given in the title of the painting. The painting is a finished object of a project in the making in the artist's studio, without assuming that the viewers agree on the meaning.

Loic Wacquant captures an important social reality of middle-class formation when he states: "The middle class is necessarily an ill-defined entity. This does not reflect a lack of theoretical penetration but rather the character of reality. Theories of the middle class should constantly strive to capture this essential ambiguity of their object rather than to dispose of it" (1991: 57). This injunction needs to be kept in mind in any attempt to establish the reality of an Istanbul new middle class.

One way to conceptualize class ambiguity is to refer to a core middle-class fragment as less ambiguously constituted than either upper middle-class or lower middle-class fragments, which necessarily share more with capital and labor, respectively. The next chapter delves more deeply into the conceptualization of the Istanbul middle class. Here the concern is to give some empirical support to the realization of an Istanbul middle class by locating it in the cityscape.

One instrument we used to locate class in social space and to refine the social construction of class by district was a socioeconomic survey undertaken in the summer of 1993. The survey was named Global Integration of Turkey's Economy and Changing Household Consumption Trends. Throughout the book, it is referred to as the 1993 Survey (see Appendix A). The survey, conducted by eight university students, was administered to 550 households scattered across 104 districts of Istanbul. One of the aims of the 1993 Survey was to discover whether our presuppositions, based in part on university students' classroom perceptions, were supported by answers to standardized survey questions. The 1993 Survey was our main instrument for ferreting out patterned relationships among occupations, attained levels of education, and consumer lifestyles.

Interviews

In 1994 we narrowed our primary focus to the significance of the annual national Selective Middle Schools Examinations (SMSEs) as a window on the rise in importance of an Istanbul new middle class and its reproduction. Balkan's lifelong associations with friends and classmates, together with his wife's extended family (*büyük aile*) provided access to persons when we conducted twenty-six taped interviews with parents, teachers, school administrators, school entrepreneurs, and tutors during the spring of 1996 (see Appendix B).

Of thirty-six adults who agreed to be taped, twenty-six were parents, four were private school owners or administrators, three were private tutors, one was a high school teacher, one a journalist who wrote an education column in a major Istanbul newspaper, and one who was a partner and administrator of a private lesson school. Nine of the parent interviews were conducted with both spouses present. In addition to taped interviews, we had innumerable informal conversations about all aspects of education with many people, educators as well as educated, over a period that spanned seven years of periodic living in Istanbul. Many of the comments and observations made during conversations found their way into a daily journal, and helped us to frame relevant topics and issues that eventually became part of the design of our interviews as well as having an influence on many other aspects of our project.

Our main interest in doing taped interviews was to accumulate a record of how families planned for the education of their children. Education plans are no casual matter. Parents begin with a plan at the birth of a child and involve a wide range of family members. We wanted their experience of their world in their words. As it turned out, this was not difficult to achieve. Working through family, friends, relatives, former students, and classmates, we were able to gain introductions to a rather wide range of new middle-class families who lived in widely separated districts of Istanbul. These introductions were invaluable, indeed necessary, to the success of our project. Had we merely selected people according to some objective criteria, the interviews would have been formal and brief. As it turned out, the interviews were lively and interactive. People had much to say about "Turkey's education system today." They discussed and debated their differences on topics such as the immorality of the state, their own ambivalent feelings of resistance and resignation toward the national middle schools examinations, the failure of public education, the sacrifices of the family, and many other topics related to success and failure, tests and education, class and privilege. They often struggled to find language that would articulate their feelings about the lost childhood of their children and to contrast it with the memory of their own experience.

Parents had much to say about schools, education, and tests. They also placed their personal experience in the larger context of relations among family, state, and market by talking personally about administrators, teachers, and tutors. We were particularly interested in education entrepreneurs who had built and operated private schools, lesson schools, or gone into business for themselves as private tutors. We were fortunate to be able to tape interviews with several of the most successful education entrepreneurs in Istanbul in each of these categories.

In the summer of 2006, Balkan conducted follow-up taped interviews to track education destinations and compare them with families' earlier aspirations, expectations, and understandings. The information obtained from interviews as well as interviewees' perspectives on various aspects of education and testing and their importance to upper middle-class families proved invaluable to our interpretation of class reproduction by means of education.

Notes

1. During the period we conducted our research (1990–1997), the selective middle school tests were given at the end of fifth grade. In the summer of 1997, the Ministry of National Education announced the Eight Grade Reform, extending compulsory comprehensive elementary education to eighth grade. The selective middle schools test was also moved to the end of eighth grade. The test was given for entrance to selective middle schools from grades nine through eleven, at the end of which lycée graduates would prepare for and take university entrance examinations. The structure and logic of the test were unchanged, but the reform altered the dynamics and strategies of families competing in the university entrance examinations to follow.
2. Nelly P. Stromquist and Karen Monkman point out that before 1997, "globalization" has been treated primarily as an economic and technological phenomenon, not within an educational or cultural perspective. Their edited volume of essays on the intersection of education and globalization is aimed at correcting this deficit. The essay by Martin Carnoy sees at least three effects of globalization that relate to the ideology of neoliberalism: the pressure on states to reduce the growth of public spending on education, shifting the burden on other sources of funding (entrepreneurs of private schools, the wealth of families, etc.), spending on higher education because it results in graduates that produce higher returns, and a focus on quality education. For these and related essays, see Stromquist and Monkman 2000.

3. One measure of a globalizing city is its rate of growth in economic output. By this measure, Istanbul is projected to work its way into the top thirty globalizing cities by the year 2020 along with Buenos Aires, Shanghai, and Mumbai (Daneshklu 2007).
4. The painting is housed in The Museum of Modern Art, New York, gift of Walter P. Chrysler, Jr., 1935.

1

Class Matters

✦

When British Prime Minister Tony Blair reputedly was asked at a press conference about the value of education in today's global economy, he is said to have responded gamely with the phrase, "the more you learn, the more you earn." The stakes of becoming middle class and reproducing class have risen, increasing the demand for cultural capital in the form of education. New middle-class families, especially in globalizing cities around the world, from London to Bombay and New York to Istanbul, have awakened to the belief that the latest round of world capitalist accumulation constitutes a fundamental shift in their ability to provide their children with what they euphemistically refer to as "a comfortable life."

We refer to those Istanbul families that are in competition with each other under conditions of globalizing neoliberal markets as a "new middle class." While there would appear to be a global trend in economic, social, and cultural differentiation within a middle class, accompanied everywhere by a middle-class crisis of access to, and affordability of, quality education, the dynamics of new middle-class formation must be understood within both national and local contexts where the agency of state, market, and family mutually shape each other. Although neoliberal capitalist ideology emphasizes enterprise free from state interference, in reality the formation of the state has always played a major role in shaping the evolution of capitalism and vice versa.[1] Their interdependence and contradictions are part of the dialectic of capitalist social formation.

The Class Analyst Is Part of Class Analysis

Early in our research, we made a decision to focus on Istanbul middle-class households and families as agents of middle-class reproduction and transformation. At first, we focused on the meaning and content of changing household consumption habits because, we reasoned, these formed a nexus of activity at the intersection of economics and culture, a meeting of our respective professional fields of inquiry. The result was a survey we conducted in 1993 of five hundred and fifty households that (1) helped us to sharpen our understanding of middle-class social space, (2) gave us a picture of changing tastes in middle-class culture, and (3) provided us with a clear view of families that comprised a new middle-class fragment that were beginning to benefit economically, socially, and culturally due to the immanent structural transformation from welfare state into neoliberal state.[2]

The survey was invaluable for locating the new middle class in districts of the city, as well as confirming characteristics of new middle-class families, but it provided little information on the dynamics of middle-class formation. This came informally through endless casual conversations with friends, colleagues, students, and families. Slowly we realized that conversation gravitated toward children and their education. The mantra of "quality education" emerged as a metadiscourse for the reproduction of social class. The discourse of quality education was interwoven with another discourse—namely, the imperative for providing their children with "a comfortable life." Together the meanings of quality and comfort framed our formal interviews that zeroed in on winning the national Selective Middle Schools tests. Money, social connections, cultural knowledge, formal schooling, and a general sophistication in the world seemed to have something to do with a determination to win the SMSEs.

The first national middle school tests were held in 1983, the iconic date for the appearance of important neoliberal reforms of the economy. The significance of these events and their meaning for the making of a new middle class are taken up in the next chapter.

Theorizing New Middle-class Formation

The French sociologist Pierre Bourdieu bridged the conceptual divide between social theory and empirical inquiry, on the one hand, and on the other by reconciling subjectivism with objectivism in an effort to form a coherent theory of practice that includes both. Thompson (1991), in his introduction to Bourdieu's *Language and Symbolic Power*, offers a succinct overview of the methodological issues that Bourdieu struggled to resolve in his earlier work:

> By 'subjectivism' Bourdieu means an intellectual orientation to the social world which seeks to grasp the way the world appears to the individuals who are situated within it. Subjectivism presupposes the possibility of some kind of immediate apprehension of the lived experience of others, and it assumes that this apprehension is by itself a more or less adequate form of knowledge about the social world . . . By 'objectivism' Bourdieu means an intellectual orientation to the social world which seeks to construct the objective relations which structure practices and representations; it places the primary experience of the social world in brackets and attempts to elucidate the structures and principles upon which primary experience depends but which it cannot directly grasp. . . . Bourdieu's view is that both subjectivism and objectivism are inadequate intellectual orientations . . . His alternative theory of practice is an attempt to move beyond objectivism without relapsing into subjectivism, that is, to take account of the need to break with immediate experience while at the same time doing justice to the practical character of social life (11–12).

While Bourdieu held onto the necessity of having an objectivist approach to social life that, by definition, was not solely dependent on the interpretation of the subjects of investigation, Loic Wacquant states that Bourdieu's guiding belief throughout his long career was the view that lived experience is constitutive of class and "cannot be directly deduced from an objectivist understanding of class structure." (Wacquant 1991: 52). He asserts that it is necessary to understand the middle class as a historical formation "through an analysis of the whole set of creative strategies . . . pursued by all the agents . . . situated at the various theoretically pertinent locations in social space" (1991: 52).

Once we take into account the subjective perspective of the class analyst in the otherwise objective analysis of class, much debate about class can be seen as having to do less with questions about what class is than with questions about the context and meaning related to issues of language and its interpretation. In other words, discursive practices of the actors need to be interrogated to interpret what it means to be new middle class and how this form of consciousness affects restructuration of the class system in place. We alluded above to different approaches that practitioners have taken to the analysis of class and the debates that have resulted over how best to do it. Mike Savage and his coauthors divide the literature into three broad categories. The first is abstract and analytical, and locates the middle class between binary relations of the capitalist and working class; the second is empirical and describes work, culture, and lifestyles in various groupings and their distinctiveness; the third has to do with theorizing middle classes as "distinct social classes in their own right" (Savage et al. 1992: 1–5).

Our approach to the appearance and reproduction of the Istanbul new middle class considers these alternatives to fall within a single methodology. Together, they constitute necessary thought processes that we have used, in no particular order, to frame our ideas, guide our research, and arrive at conclusions.

We interrogate the education system as an objective phenomenon in which we explore the rules and regulations of a field of competitive social relations created, controlled, and regulated by an office of the Ministry of National Education. To understand the practices of agents that provide market services and families that plan their children's education and prepare for the SMSEs, we needed to explore Wacquant's "whole set of strategies pursued by the agents" (1991: 52).

Accumulation, Multiple Capitals, and the Reproduction of the Istanbul New Class

Bourdieu views the social world as one of accumulated history, "and if it is not to be reduced to a discontinuous series of instantaneous mechanical equilibria between agents who are treated as interchangeable particles, one must reintroduce into it the notion of capital and with it, accumulation and all its effects." (Bourdieu 1997: 46) *Capital* denotes any materials, knowledge, or ideas used to produce, transport, create, or alter commodities for the purpose of accumulation. Marketable intangibles, or what we refer to as *symbolic capital*, such as credit, promises, good will, copyrights, brand names, trademarks, patents, stocks, bonds, and franchises are among the items included as instruments of capital accumulation. Bourdieu (1997: 46–58) distinguishes among three forms of capital for purposes of analysis. The first he labels *economic capital*, "which is immediately and directly convertible into money and may be institutionalized in the form of property rights." The second is *cultural capital*, "which is convertible, on certain conditions, into economic capital and may be institutionalized in the form of educational qualifications." The third is *social capital*, defined as "the aggregate of the actual or potential resources which are linked to possession of a durable network of more or less institutionalized relationships of mutual acquaintance and recognition [that] provides each of its members with the backing of collectively-owned capital as actual and potential credit." With regard to Bourdieu's institutionalization of the forms of capital, economic capital is institutionalized as "property rights," cultural capital as "education qualifications," and social capital as "durable networks."

In this classification, the principles that structure each form of capital fit into three kinds of stipulation: convertibility, ownership, and norms. The first is stipulations about what governs convertibility from one form of capital to another. The second is stipulations about what constitutes ownership of capital. The third is about sociability or moral norms that confer credit and incur debt. The main point is that material, cultural, and social resources can become forms of capital that vary widely in their historically specific institutionalization of convertibility, property rights, and moral norms. They are present in all historical social formations that include state, market, and family, and serve to locate and delineate different forms of value as different spheres of value formation.

As a working definition that reflects the scope of exchange in the social world, we define *capital* as any object or idea that can be used to augment "value" through exchange and conversion. Put this way, the problem becomes how to reconcile apparently incommensurable values with the empirical realities of their variable forms of exchange and convertibility.[3] The economy, in the narrow sense of market prices, is embedded in the larger social world of value formation in which class reproduction is part of an accumulation history of any chosen entity. We argue that families are the proximate agents of middle-class reproduction in Istanbul, and it is their particular accumulation histories that need to be explored in an effort to understand the education strategies of a new middle class. *Class formation* refers to those exchange practices most closely associated with the accumulation of multiple capitals, with special emphasis on cultural capital—particularly in a competitive field of social relations that were structured by the state through its imposition of a selective system of tests that forced new middle-class families to compete for places in the best middle schools.

During the 1990s, cultural industries, including both cultural products and cultural property, constituted one of the fastest-growing sectors in the global capitalist economy. The commoditization of culture represented the decoupling of cultural capital from its previous irreducible social and cultural principles, thereby increasing the probability of converting cultural values into capitalist market value.

Cultural capital appears in three forms: *embodied*, *objectified*, and *institutionalized*. In its embodied state, it appears in the form of enduring dispositions of the mind and body of a person. In its objectified state, it appears in the form of cultural goods such as books or paintings, which are the traces of the ideas, theories, interpretations, critiques, puzzles, or problematics that are recognized publicly and collectively as knowledge. In its institutionalized state, it appears as "a form of objectification which must be set apart because it confers entirely original properties on the cultural capital which it is presumed to guarantee" (Bourdieu 1997: 47). Bourdieu's example is educational qualifications such as certification and credentialing, representations of cultural capital that are central to the subject of this book. The different capitals are not mutually exclusive. From the perspective of practices, any or all types may be implicated in the strategy options of families competing to win the SMSEs. These remain empirical problems to be subjected to scrutiny and interpretation in the last chapters of the book.

Information and knowledge gained through popular culture is a different form of cultural capital from that acquired through formal education. They are objectified in different ways. The accumulation of education credentials in all their forms create sharper distinctions than, say, the distinction conferred on taste. Language is a vehicle for symbolic interpretation of all the capitals but also can serve as a more defined class marker than other media. All the forms of cultural capital have their own principles governing their forms of value but also possess the potential of being converted into each other in the service of reproducing the new middle class. Certain foreign languages that are associated with specific schools in Istanbul, for example, are among the most important markers of elitism sought after by upper middle-class families and hold a near absolute value for them. They also can be converted into an economic value when their credentials are priced in the labor market. They acquire additional symbolic value when converted into social capital that adds to the prestige and privilege accorded them by society. Cultural capital is used to reinforce other principles of social inclusion and exclusion.

Accumulation is a process that is segmented into different institutionalized spheres, each with its own rules, such as social networks of families, an organized system of schools and education, and an organized capitalist labor market. These spheres can also be conceptualized as different fields of competitive relations in which families of similar class compete with each other in a struggle that reproduces the class as an entity. Our focus is on the competitive field of education, specifically the state-controlled national competition for places in the best middle schools in Turkey, many of which are in Istanbul.

Our purpose in using the concept of cultural capital to frame issues in middle-class formation by means of education is to explore embodied, objectified, and institutionalized practices similar to the ones that first motivated Bourdieu, namely, an analysis of the state's hegemony over access to elite education and its relation to the reproduction of a new social class. Our aim will be to elucidate the relationships among cultural capital, its conversion into educational qualifications, and the social basis of class solidarity in Istanbul during this era of economic globalization.

In a capitalist society, economic capital is hegemonic. Economic logic dominates as a cultural ideology because the tendency is toward conversion of all forms of value into that of the capitalist market, symbolized by money, a commodity that stands for the value of all other commodities but which has no use value of its own. Bourdieu acknowledges the domination of economic capital in a capitalist society when he argues that social and cultural capitals function as disguised forms of economic capital. But he goes on to say that cultural and social capitals are "never entirely reducible" to economic capital (1997: 54). The tautological reason he gives is that social and cultural capitals have their own respective "efficacies." We would add that they have their own socially bounded spheres of valuation, rules of exchange and communication, and institutionalization. It remains an empirical question whether these capitals perform the function of hiding economic capital, presumably because of the dangers associated with revealing class relations of inequality.

The social world is indeed a world of accumulated history. In the context of middle-class formation in Istanbul, to be or become an upper middle-class family requires not only material wealth but also social and cultural capital. Cultural capital in its objectified and embodied form of education and certification of individuals requires long-term collective planning and execution. It begins at birth with a plan for an education path that leads to a top university. From the standpoint of the multicapitalized family and its middle-class norms, employment follows education, marriage follows employment, and family follows all three in the life course. The sequence is enacted through many conversions of the forms of capital. The long march of family members, or embodied capital, from primary school to university is the sine qua non of a process of accumulation that is meant to ensure not only the reproduction of the person but also the reproduction of the family as upper middle class. Person, family, and class are mutually constituted through multiple capital conversions and the practices associated with them.

Notes

1. See Karl Polanyi's class work, *The Great Transformation* (1944).
2. Bronwyn Davies and Peter Bansel (2007) explore how qualitative studies fit into the discourses and practices of neoliberalism in ways that enable us to understand state policies toward education and how they affect the making of a new middle class.
3. For issues related to spheres of social and economic exchange and how different forms of value are converted from one to another in different societies, see Sahlins 1965. For historical examples of the same issues, see Polanyi, Erensberg, and Pearson 1957.

2

THE NEOLIBERAL LANDSCAPE

A coup in 1980 marked the end of national developmentalism in Turkey and the beginning of the country's liberalization episode. The aim was to remove trade barriers in order to increase the rate of economic growth through an export-oriented strategy aimed at entry into global markets. By 1980, Turkey had a modern class structure built on the foundation of a combination of state-owned and state-guided private enterprises. There was a thriving national market for consumer goods produced by Turkish manufacturers and nursed by state promotion of a cultural ideology of consumption. The captains of industry had achieved the status of a national bourgeoisie, which, in turn, had come to rely upon the entrepreneurial, managerial, technical, and professional services of an urban, university-educated upper middle class. The core fragments of the middle class consisted of the *salariat*, which distinguished families of the middle class from a class of wage earners and those who held the means of production. By 1980, the core middle-class family could expect a comfortable life, secured by state provisioning of health, education, and pensions.

In the decades prior to 1980, the families of middle and upper middle-class fragments seemed to share consumption habits anchored in twin aspirations of living "a comfortable life" and attaining higher education. Perceived differences were embedded in a shared structure of feeling that the lives of their children would be better than theirs. In other words, the idea of improving class by means of education was common to both fragments of the middle class, belying the reality of the privileges already enjoyed by the established upper middle class.

The characteristics of and distinctions within the middle class of the post-1980 era in Turkey might best be understood within the context of the forces of global neoliberalism shaping developing economies. Over the past several decades, in one country after another, the logic of the globalizing market exerted pressure on nation-states to make wide-ranging policy changes favorable to free trade and economic growth. The policy of solving national problems through growth in capital opened virtually every sector of the national economy to the forces of global capitalist markets. Direct investment by foreign corporations became, in the eyes of many analysts, the most efficient cure for all social, political, and economic problems. This neoliberal perspective on the problems of the nation-state found an audience in almost every developing nation across the globe.[1] The ideology of neoliberalism, as globalized free enterprise came to be called, pro-claimed national borders to be an obstruction to the free flow of global information and ideas, technological innovation, goods, people (labor), and financial capital—all factors critical to other forms of social and cultural development. Under the increasing pressures of neoliberal ideology and policy-makers, national governments came to be viewed as imposing an unbearable regulatory burden on individual initiative and a tax on collective welfare. Removing such obstacles would unleash human creativity and wealth, and also would bring a rising tide of wealth to all countries and all classes of people. These economic suppositions went hand in hand with the political claim that opening national markets to global trade and capital would bring not only the benefits of efficiency but also the elusive blessings of equity. The rising tide of global capital would raise all boats. People of every country, eventually and inevitably, would be better off in the new global marketplace.

Liberalization and the Restructuring of the Turkish Economy

Turkey participated in this project of neoliberal reforms. Its liberalization episode, which embodied the ideas of free-market benefits, began with an economic and political crisis in 1979 following a decade of turmoil between the Turkish political left and right. This crisis culminated in major bottlenecks in the economy, a slowdown of growth, a very high rate of inflation, high accumulation of external debts, and serious social unrest and street violence that resulted in thousands of deaths. A solution to the crisis that would help stabilize the Turkish monetary system was agreed upon between the Turkish government and the International Monetary Fund (IMF). On January 24, 1980, the government introduced a comprehensive economic stabilization program.[2] The major elements of the reform program, aimed at deregulating markets and opening them to competition, were as follows: the gradual removal of trade restrictions towards full commodity trade liberalization, the liberalization of the interest rates and the exchange rate regime, the privatization of industries and public services such as education, and the elimination of price controls and subsidies. This was followed throughout the 1980s by complete financial liberalization. The state abruptly abandoned national developmentalist policies.

A new government established in 1983[3] announced that it would reinforce the economic policies initiated in 1980 by introducing a greater degree of liberalization, minimizing the role of the state in regulating markets, and reducing what was perceived to be excessive intervention in the economy.

The historical role of state policies in redistributing resources vital to class formation now took a different turn, one that not only changed the national distribution of economic capital but also changed the social contract between the state and the middle class. In order to understand how this happened, and what it meant for middle-class economic and social reproduction, it is necessary to grasp, through various questions, the underlying economic and cultural logic of state policies that give substance to such concepts as liberalization, deregulation, privatization, and crisis. What was the state's main motivation behind liberalization and what were its main objectives? What were the consequences of the liberalization episode on different classes in the economy? How was the existing middle class hollowed out and polarized, resulting in a small but growing urban, professional, highly educated and globally linked fraction that have come to be known in the academic and media discourses as the new middle class? This chapter addresses the underlying causes leading to the bifurcation within the middle class as a result of neoliberal policies and the appearance of the new middle class in the Istanbul neoliberal landscape.

Accumulation by Dispossession

Marxist geographer David Harvey, in *A Brief History of Neoliberalism*, argues that "neoliberalism is in the first instance a theory of political economic practices that proposes that human well-being can best be advanced by liberating individual entrepreneurial freedoms and skills within an institutional framework characterized by strong private property rights, free markets, and free trade" (2005: 3). In order to secure this neoliberal framework, the state "must also set those military, defense, police, and legal structures and functions required to secure private property rights and guarantee, by force if need be, the proper functioning of markets. Furthermore, if markets do not exist (in areas such as land, water, education, health care, social security, or environmental pollution) then they must be created, by state action if necessary" (2005: 3). Harvey's analysis of the new round of capital accumulation rests on the concept of "accumulation by dispossession" (2003: 137–83). This means opening up new areas for capital accumulation either by selling off state (public) assets or by forcing the governments to privatize, commodify, and marketize areas of social life that previously resisted the logic of capital. It also means state manipulation of crises and state redistribution of wealth and income through various policies. This process "has, however, entailed much 'creative destruction', not only of prior institutional frameworks and powers but also of divisions of labor, social relations, welfare provisions, technological mixes, ways of life and thought, reproductive activities, attachments to land and habits of the heart" (2005: 3). In fact, at the heart of the neoliberal ideology is this basic logic of capital.

Policies of Accumulation by Dispossession

During the neoliberal era, certain policies of dispossession such as state redistribution, financialization, and privatization created a new middle class in the globally integrated and fast growing economic sectors like exports, financial services, banking, tourism, media, advertising, accounting, and entertainment. An increasing number of highly educated professionals were able to situate themselves favorably in various sectors of the fast-track economy, accumulating assets and real wealth and thereby experiencing rapid upward material mobility. This group stood to gain the most ground, economically and politically, in ways that not only reproduced their class position but also elevated it—one is tempted to say *leveraged* it—in relation to the rest of the middle class. Income gaps *within* the middle class continued to widen.

State Redistribution

The liberalization period witnessed a dramatic change in the role of the state. The state shifted missions, from being a provider of social benefits and social investments to a regulator of income distribution in the interest of capital. The state redistribution of income was implemented through various policy tools such as devaluation, interest rate manipulation, public borrowing, and taxation.

One of the first neoliberal policies was the devaluation of the Turkish lira to boost exports. Later, in 1989, all restrictions on foreign exchange were lifted and the Turkish lira became fully convertible. This also meant that capital flows would be totally unregulated.

By a devaluation of its currency, a government hopes to generate more foreign demand for its goods while reducing the demand for imports, thereby improving the country's trade balance. Devaluation has the immediate effect of raising prices of imported goods in terms of the local currency. Imported goods—cars, textiles, and electronic devices, for instance—will cost more.

There are severe distributional effects of devaluations in the domestic economy. By changing the domestic prices of exports and imports and creating incentives for the exporting sectors (tradables) as opposed to domestic goods (nontradables), devaluation will benefit certain groups at the expense of others. In general, urban wage and salary earners, people with fixed incomes, small farmers, and rural and urban small-scale producers and suppliers of services who do not participate in the exporting sector suffer from the domestic inflation that typically follows devaluation. Their consumption is lowered through a decline in wages and salaries in order that a surplus of goods for export can be created. Meanwhile those in the export sector gain. The more the ownership of and control over the export sector are concentrated in private hands, the greater is the effect of devaluation on income distribution.

One other form of state redistribution was implemented through the manipulation of interest rates. The government of Turgut Özal had made promises to improve the purchasing power and saving capacity of the middle class and to ease the acute housing shortage through special incentives and programs. While talking about these reforms, he used the word "*ortadirek*" to refer to the middle class, a term meaning the "core structure, pole or pillar" of a tent, as a rhetorical device to signal an intention to restore the economic base and social welfare of the middle class following the 1979 crisis.

In line with this rhetoric and in keeping with this program, Özal's government declared a "war" on inflation as the primary animus of its multipronged program. He promised to reduce the inflation rate in an effort to stop the erosion of middle-class purchasing power and savings. Once the inflation rate was reduced, middle-class incomes would rise and income distribution would equalize, favoring this class.

To achieve this goal, the government reasoned, it would be necessary to liberalize interest rates. As interest rates went up, the middle class would put lifetime savings into time deposit bank accounts, creating a tool for increasing income. Increased savings would reduce consumption and therefore inflation. Upper middle-class families that were losing real income due to the high inflation rate by the end of the 1970s received this policy warmly as well.

Prior to this era, savings accounts were not very common among middle-class households because of negative real interest rates on time deposit accounts. Middle-class families kept their savings in the form of gold or real estate. At first, interest rate liberalization resulted in a fierce struggle among banks and broker institutions to attract funds from the public, mainly middle-class households. Unfortunately, this option was short lived due to a banking crisis in 1982. Kastelli, the largest broker, became insolvent and fled the country, leaving long lines in front of his brokerage houses. Middle-class people who had sold their houses or gold and deposited the proceeds with the bankers were the main losers. Although it is not known how many households lost their savings in this episode, it is clear that this first encounter with unregulated global capitalist markets was a disaster for the middle class, the supposed beneficiaries of the new policy. Following these failures, the government returned to its policy of regulating deposit rates, but in 1987, it liberalized interest rates again and banks were allowed to determine rates for their deposits. Once again middle-class families began to keep their savings in the form of high-interest deposit accounts in order to stretch their continuously shrinking incomes due to inflation.

The distribution and size of deposits revealed the winners of this policy.[4] The overall effect was to increase the rent income of a very small number of deposit holders. Those who had substantial savings, like the capitalists and upper middle-class families, were able to increase their income through interest earnings. But for the vast majority, things only got worse. The majority of core middle-class families lost their purchasing power as a result of interest rate manipulation.[5]

The failed promise of improving the income of the vast majority of middle-class families had the effect of placing them at greater risk with an increasingly uncertain future. Economic uncertainty, though, was not the only concern. In the old system, the middle-class families had a respected status in Turkish society. Their social worth seemed to be assured. Now it was being undermined.

One other form of state redistribution of income was implemented through public borrowing, by transferring income to holders of public debt instruments (mainly the rentiers and the financial sector) through interest payments. Persistent and high inflation had created incentives for the private sector to delay tax and social security payments. The system encouraged evasion. Firms withheld these payments and invested them in government bonds earning high profits because the return on government bonds was far greater than the penalty they paid for being behind in their payments.

Meanwhile, tax policies favoring capital and punishing labor were continued. There was a shift from an earlier progressive income tax to an almost regressive one, favoring dividend and interest income on government bonds and treasury bills and increasing the tax burden on wage and salary earners. In addition, capital gains on real estate and financial assets were all exempted from taxation. These exemptions allowed an avenue of rapid accumulation for the new middle class who invested in the urban real estate boom, especially in Istanbul. Intellectual-property incomes and interest revenues on bank deposits were taxed at flat rates much lower than the lowest tax bracket applicable to wages and salaries.[6]

Financialization and the Istanbul Stock Exchange

The Istanbul Stock Exchange (ISE) was initiated in 1986 and a Capital Market Board was established in order to regulate and supervise the capital market. The removal of all restrictions on capital flows completed the financial liberalization program. An important characteristic of this final phase of liberalization was the massive flow of short-term speculative capital in response to fluctuations in exchange rates and interest rates. There were three sources of hot-money movements that dominated the capital account and led to external debt growth during this period: rentiers, firms, and banks. Rentiers engaged in currency switching, mostly between dollar and Turkish Lira (TL) assets, capital flight, and its reversal. Firms shifted between borrowing in TL and foreign currency. Banks borrowed abroad and lent domestically. In 1993, the Turkish stock market was considered to be one of the best-performing emerging stock markets in the world.

Growth in the financial sector is one of the clearest indications not only of higher incomes but also of the prospect for wealth that is one of the characteristics of the new middle class. Financial markets, including operations of the ISE, were the source of many new occupations as well as investment opportunities sought by the new middle class.

A series of reforms were undertaken in Turkey's capital markets that clearly advantaged this emerging new middle class. An interbank money market law was enacted in 1986. Significant tax incentives were conferred on the financial sector to encourage equity financing. This policy benefited the new middle class at a time when core middle-class wage and salary earners already were carrying a disproportionate share of taxes. Also, the creation of the credit card industry enhanced the economic power and stature of the new middle class by enabling increased consumption.

In 1994, the government's attempts to reduce interest rates resulted in a massive outflow of short-term capital, necessitating a 65 percent devaluation of the Turkish lira. The financial crisis was, in part, a result of deteriorating macroeconomic fundamentals that were rooted in public sector imbalances. Important consequences of the currency crisis were the decimation of middle-class savings due to devaluation and high inflation, and the worsening of income distribution.

The currency crisis led to the implementation of an austerity program in April 1994. Fiscal "belt tightening" had the aim of restoring confidence in the domestic currency, reducing fiscal and external imbalances through cutbacks in government social spending, and forcing a slowdown of inflation. These structural adjustments had their effect on realignments within middle-class fragments that reflected a global shift in wealth, power, and privilege. The new middle class diverged from the core middle class, resembling a capitalist class more and more, while the core middle class, in turn, began to resemble the lower middle and upper working classes. Social bifurcation within the middle class continued during the postcrisis years.

Privatization and Commodification

The privatization of public assets has been an important feature of neoliberalism. In both industrialized and developing countries, state enterprises and banks, public utilities of all kinds (water, telecommunications, transportation), social welfare provisions (social housing, education, health care, pensions), public institutions (for example universities), and public land have been privatized to some degree.

Under neoliberalism, Turkey had its share of privatization as well. Privatization implementations gained momentum in 1986, and since then 193 companies have been privatized. Currently, the state does not have any ownership in 184 of these companies. The state completely withdrew from the cement, animal feed production, dairy products, forest products, ground handling, catering services, and petroleum distribution sectors. More than 50 percent of the state shares were privatized in tourism, iron and steel, textiles, sea freight, and meat processing sectors. The state has partially withdrawn from the ports and petroleum refinery sector. Privatization of public banks has commenced with Sümerbank and continued with Etibank, Denizbank, and Anadolu Bank. Public utilities like telecommunications and transportation were also opened to the private sector (YASED 2006: 20–22).

Privatization of public enterprises had major effects on middle-class families. Those who worked for the public sector lost their jobs and had a hard time finding new employment with similar salaries and benefits, given the high unemployment rates in the economy. Meanwhile, because public enterprises and services were privatized, middle-class families lost their access to affordable subsidized goods and services. Both developments led to the erosion of middle-class purchasing power.

Privatization affected social welfare provisions as well. Education, health care, and social security all experienced lower public investments under liberalization. Throughout the 1980s, the ratio of public spending on education and health services to gross domestic product showed a continuous downward trend. The withdrawal of the state from the provision of these services led to their commodification. From 1994 on, private investors started moving into these sectors due to generous government incentives. By 1996–97, the private sector's share in total education and health investments reached 50 percent (Boratav et al. 1995: 359). An expensive and in many ways luxurious private health care system emerged alongside the overextended public health system. The private system was supported by private health insurance schemes while public health care suffered from lack of public spending. This dual system clearly demonstrated the polarization of service delivery in the society. The core middle class was limited with insufficient public services due to loss of income, while the emerging new middle class enjoyed the benefits of the expensive private system. Within recent collective memory, social benefits and services that had been proclaimed by the government as the welfare of the *ortadirek* had become costs on capital accumulation and the pursuit of free enterprise.

In conclusion, during the neoliberal era of capital accumulation by dispossession, many professionals and businessmen of the Turkish "new economy" utilized their education and social connections to become part of the global "new economy," which was constantly creating new demand for specific occupations that required special individuals with special education. Speaking a foreign language, having a degree from a prestigious university (often abroad), being interested in the business culture, cultivating certain consumption habits, and being ready to adopt (or at least adapt to) "the American way of life" or its French or German variants were among the most desired qualities for success in the new economy.

State enterprises, however, were slow to change, and most of the core middle-class professionals, managers, and technicians worked for public institutions or state-owned enterprises. State employees differed in wages and other material and social capitals from their counterparts in the private sector and lacked the entrepreneurial credentials and opportunistic predispositions sought by the new economy. Many were not positioned to take advantage of the opportunities being generated by fast-track growth. They remained ideologically committed to national developmentalism and viewed capitalist ideology with some suspicion.

The Neoliberal Landscape in Istanbul

As described above, national middle classes are becoming more differentiated as a consequence of the new economy, new wealth, and lifestyles that reflect the ideology of the global consumer culture. The significance of the emerging global new middle classes is that they represent a new historical phase of capitalist accumulation that differentiates them from national upper middle classes of the past. They move "closer" to capital than to labor by means of participating more in the process of accumulating capital and less in their reliance on salary. They are stakeholders in the new economy and demonstrate the aspirations more of an upper class than of an industrial core middle class.

In every country, some cities more than others are involved in the organizations and networks of the global economy. At the same time, these cities are embedded in national aspirations and subject to regulation by the state. In Turkey, Istanbul, a major commercial and financial center, has emerged as the country's globalizing city. What follows is an attempt to establish the appearance of a historically particular new middle class in Istanbul as a consequence of the liberalization of the Turkish economy. Taking into account the relationships among state, market, and family institutions in class formation, the substantive areas of emphasis will be on cultural capital in the forms of lifestyle and material capital in the form of housing.

Nowhere in Turkey was the middle class more affected by neoliberal ideology and policies than in Istanbul, a world city that after 1980 became a globalizing city. How did Istanbul become a globalizing city, and how did a conjunction of global, national, and local forces contribute to the remaking of a fragment of the upper middle class as a new middle class? In the last two decades of the twentieth century, Istanbul underwent an economic revival and cultural transformation as the central location of Turkey's integration into the global economy. It became a globalizing city, the center of changes in transnational networks of foreign capital, currency exchange, import-export trade, media and communications, and technology that emanated from other parts of the world. A key part of this transformation was the appearance of a new cosmopolitanism, reflected in an outward-looking new middle class that was entrepreneurial in spirit, quick to embrace the cultural ideology of consuming everything foreign, and engrossed in postmodern preoccupations with the deconstruction of old identities in the interest of creating new ones.

Globalizing Cityscapes

While Turgut Özal's Motherland Party pursued the political strategy of urban populism to win the national election in Istanbul, one of its members, Mayor Bedrettin Dalan, pursued an economic strategy more in tune with the Motherland Party's liberalization strategy for global integration. The two strategies worked in tandem to reshape Istanbul's cityscape during the 1980s. The Ankara government set the parameters by changing the administration of metropolitan government, passing legislation that created new channels of funding to pursue a variety of urban renewal projects, and instituting the National Housing and Investment Administration, which through the Mass Housing Fund underwrote the enormous expansion of Istanbul real estate markets. Perhaps as important as any of these policies was Dalan's vision of Istanbul as an international city and his ability to articulate his vision in a way that mobilized business interest groups to enact it.

The Motherland government began to increase progressively the proportion of total tax revenues allocated to municipal administrations. In 1983, new legal provisions also allowed metropolitan governments to levy and or increase local taxes, fees, and charges on activities ranging from sports and entertainment to advertising. These activities were among the growth sectors of the urban economy. Increases in tax revenue not only allowed the city to undertake projects to improve physical infrastructure but it also financed a new fleet of buses and imported new passenger ships at a time when the center city was becoming more congested from increased automobile traffic (Keyder and Öncü 1993: 26). In 1984, the Motherland Party enacted a law designed to centralize major metropolis-wide functions and place them under the direct control and authority of the metropolitan mayor.

The Globalizing Cityscape 1: Commodification of Culture as Heritage

Mayor Dalan's economic strategy for globalizing Istanbul reflected his vision of an international city that would attract conferences and tourists from all over the world. But his vision extended beyond the usual trade and commerce industries to wed economic prosperity to cultural industries by imagining past history as heritage, an accumulation history of eleven centuries of Byzantine Constantinople followed by five centuries of Ottoman Istanbul as centers of world power and commerce. Business groups supported his initiatives, which included new highways, under- and overpasses, and clearance and beautification projects.

The historical peninsula at the confluence of the Bosphorus Strait and the Sea of Marmara had been a destination of foreign tourists for a long period, but Dalan used heritage to promote the assets of two world cities as the cultural capital of a globalizing city. The culture industries of London, New York, and other global cities were being recognized as assets of inestimable market value for attracting global corporate headquarters as well as symbolic value in their global images. In Istanbul, a vital past is present and visible within the borders of the western peninsula. Topkapı, commonly referred to as the Ottoman sultans' "palace," is an imperial city that rests on a promontory overlooking the Sea of Marmara. Before it became the home of Ottoman sultans for nearly five centuries, it was the home of Byzantine emperors for a thousand years. While much of Byzantium was ruined by the time of the Ottoman conquest in 1453, to the trained eye a surprising amount of Byzantine architecture remains intact.

Coexisting with and dominating the historical cityscape is the monumental architecture of the Ottoman period. Topkapı's walls and gates and the many buildings that housed the treasury, the enormous kitchens, the harem, and the palace itself occupy the point of the peninsula. The imperial treasures remain in the various buildings. Sultans' mosques on hilltops overlooking the Golden Horn dominate the sight line of the peninsula. The intricate pattern of lacework streets and narrow alleys that surround the museums, palaces, mosques, and monuments house one of the most densely packed residential populations in metropolitan Istanbul.

There is, then, a material presence of cosmopolitan heritage that has become a symbolic currency in efforts to reimagine Istanbul as a globalizing city. The heritage movement is also important to the story of a globalizing city in another way. It was through the tourist gaze that the city's inhabitants, especially its upper middle class, began to imagine itself as a city that was on the move, able to visualize the prospect of a bright future as continuous with a glorious past. Nearly all the physical structures that have been mentioned are in use today.

The historical peninsula also represents the deep past as present in the lives of Istanbullus. Foreign visitors and tourists who come to the historical peninsula have no choice but to intermingle with Turks from all over the metropolis who live, work, trade, and shop there. The historical peninsula remains the symbolic and physical center of the city, alive with every activity, sight, sound, and smell.

The Globalizing Cityscape 2: Financialization

If the strong presence of global financial institutions is an indicator of a globalizing city, then Istanbul met the test. By the early 1990s, a glass city that became the home of the fledgling Turkish stock market, investment banks, insurance carriers, and five-star international business hotels could be seen a few miles to the north of the old city center, just over the hills from the Bosphorus shore and minutes from the intersection of highways that brought workers over the bridge from the Asian side to merge with the traffic caused by the north-south commuters on the western side. Maslak, as the new financial area was called, became the headquarters of some of the largest Turkish transnational corporations and banks. The rapid change was dramatic when contrasted to the preexisting 1930s state banks headquartered mostly in the central Anatolian capital of Ankara to be close to the state bureaucracy that regulated them, a pattern the early private banks followed from 1950 to 1980. The Turkish Lira was not yet traded on international currency markets, and most banks in Turkey were state enterprises, each with a designated function in different development sectors of the national economy such as agriculture, social security, insurance, and maritime shipping.

The monopoly of the Central Bank over foreign currency transactions came to an end when commercial banks were freed from government regulations and able to operate in international markets, in some cases forming joint ventures with foreign banks. After 1983 there was a premium on banks with greater access to world markets. The export boom and borrowing from abroad brought foreign capital into the Istanbul economy and, more particularly, into the households of those business families that were in a position to benefit from investment in growth sectors such as finance, insurance, real estate, accounting, media, entertainment and fashion, marketing and advertising, and textiles.

New five-star international hotels catering to businessmen, conventioneers, and groups of tourists appeared in the new financial center but also in other parts of the city. Istanbul had no modern international hotel until 1955 when the Hilton was built on Cumhuriyet Boulevard near Taksim square, a center for foreign travelers and international tourism since the mid-nineteenth century. The following year the exclusive Divan Hotel was built a few blocks away. Two decades would pass before the Sheraton and Marmara hotels were added to the rising skyline around Taksim. In contrast, the decade after 1982 saw the construction of a large number of international hotels, several of which were located near corporate headquarters in the financial district.

The Globalizing Cityscape 3: Privatization of Media and Communications

The political economy and culture of media and communications was revolutionized during the liberalization episode. From three state television stations with content provided by state-funded programming before 1983, this whole industry became privatized by the early 1990s.

During the first decade of liberalization, the number of telephone subscribers increased sixfold (from 1.1 to 5.9 million). Istanbul's antiquated telephone system, which had resulted in waits of as long as fifteen years for a telephone installation, was upgraded and the wait for telephone subscribers was reduced to a matter of days. Turks make maximal use of phone communication to keep in constant contact with family, friends, and business associates. The explosion in cellular phone communication has had a dramatic impact in a city where long lines form in front of scarce phone booths.[7] The purchase and use of personal computers, fax machines, and email grew rapidly and created electronic networks for a Turkish new middle class that, quite literally, could view itself as part of an emerging global new middle class.[8]

Print and electronic media that introduced international perspectives in words and images began to have a powerful influence on public opinion but also on collective self-awareness. Satellite television introduced Istanbul audiences to programming that ranged from Mexican and Brazilian soap operas to sitcoms from European countries, influencing trends in consumer culture and delivering Turkish audiences to advertisers of a wide range of imported products and their local knock-offs. There was an explosion in the number of glossy magazines on everything from fashion, food, and entertainment to home decoration, gardening, and adventure travel. Before 1980, the government imposed travel restrictions on Turkish citizens who desired to travel abroad. By the 1990s, the flashy images of well-dressed, well-coiffured Turks in expensive holiday homes, resorts, and cars provided the underlying self-confirmation of the cultural ideology of new middle-class consumers. There was a boom in the travel industry as Turks were taking packaged tours to major tourist destinations in Latin America, the United States, Europe, and Central Asia. The international flow of people to and from Turkey was significant in forming new tastes and consumer habits. Nearly three million Turkish citizens traveled abroad by 1990, up from a little over one million in 1979. Five and a half million foreign tourists were pouring into Turkey by 1990, up from one million in 1979 (Toprak 1995: 1–3).

Distance and Difference: A Parting of Ways

Nowhere was the polarization within the middle class more visible than in the appreciation of residential real estate and the geographical separation of new middle-class housing from the housing of other middle-class fractions. The spatial separation within middle-class housing that further differentiated new and upper middle-class housing from the rest of the middle class was carried out during the real estate boom of the 1990s. Skyrocketing residential real estate prices on the high end of the market was the defining factor.

How were new middle-class households able to distance themselves spatially and differentiate themselves socially from other middle-class households? The new middle-class households whose heads were employed in growing sectors of the privatized economy such as banking, insurance, accounting, real estate, advertising, marketing, medicine, information technology, media and entertainment, tourism, and export trade had many opportunities for accumulating assets and wealth.

These households avoided the effects of taxation and inflation imposed on fixed-income earners by receiving profits on export subsidies and speculative profits through currency transactions. They held large foreign currency deposit accounts that allowed them to avoid the effects of inflation on the erosion of the Turkish lira, and they enjoyed the rewards of tax-free capital gains from property and equity investments. Meanwhile, households of the core and lower middle-class fractions had taxes taken out of their wages and salaries at the source. New middle-class families were also in a position to purchase private health care and health insurance. Households of the core and lower middle class had to receive their healthcare from overworked and underpaid doctors and overcrowded and underfunded state hospitals. The result was increasing social differentiation that, in the context of the real estate boom, inevitably meant greater spatial separation between new middle-class spaces and those of other middle-class fragments.

New middle-class households that were able to earn windfall profits and shield themselves from high inflation and taxation were in a position to move up in housing with greater material comfort in a development with more amenities. The real estate developers responded with offerings of luxurious gated communities that had every conceivable amenity and service within its walls, creating the appearance of multiple fortifications within the surrounding spaces of new high-rise apartment buildings. The irony of new middle-class fortifications in a city of decayed ancient fortifications was not lost on social commentators.

The general middle-class trend in sociogeographical mobility from nonrandom data in the 1993 Survey can be summarized as follows. Immobility was modal. One of the underlying reasons for no or low mobility was an appreciation of market prices that placed middle-class households at a relative disadvantage when the apartment they sold would be worth less than the money needed to buy a new one. Core middle-class households on fixed incomes with little chance for savings to invest in the purchase of housing would be one group that fit the pattern of geographical immobility. But upward mobility was also modal, especially among those households who by 1993 could take advantage of export subsidies and capital gains laws while avoiding the worst effects of inflation on income and savings. The 1993 Survey provides evidence of some social mobility across class fractions. Households in the highest rent neighborhoods in 1993 that had moved there since 1980 were, in nearly equal numbers, from high, moderate, and lower rent neighborhoods. Likewise, a number of households that resided in moderately priced neighborhoods in 1993 had moved from lower and low-priced neighborhoods.

There was more to Istanbul new middle-class living arrangements than social differentiation by spatial separation, the added value of appreciating real estate prices, and quick access to workplaces and shopping centers via motorways and beltways. As more public projects focused on rapid transportation and public parks, more private capital flowed into the housing market to meet growing demand for "naturalized" site locations, stylish exterior and interior design, and consumer services of all kinds. Outdoor amenities such as planted miniature forests, lawns, gardens, fountains, and pathways became more common in the spaces on the edge of the city. The appearance of artificial lakes, recreation areas, and health clubs were responses to a new awareness of, and fascination with, the body. The new middle class led the way. With money came more choice, and with more choice came more self-conscious identity play with consumer lifestyles from many foreign countries. It was the actuality of the global ideology of consumer culture in the social spaces of Istanbul that turned older cosmopolitan ways into new globalizing lifestyles. The new middle class could gaze at a plethora of billboards, television personalities, and slick magazine advertisements as if they were seeing themselves through a looking glass. Advertising and media set out to deliver products that were designed to satisfy the desire to gaze at others and be a part of the scene. There was an equally strong urge to be private and exclusive. In a world of commodified culture, all things seem possible.

There are at least two commodity aesthetics at work to produce new middle-class living arrangements in globalizing cities such as Istanbul. The first we might call *commodity cosmopolitanism*, fueled by the desire to be surrounded by new upscale shopping centers and boulevards, cinema complexes, ethnic restaurants, coffee houses, art galleries, museums, and other sites for culture and leisure such as yacht harbors, health and athletic centers, bistros, and social clubs. Being surrounded by "a dense jungle" of places for pleasure and leisure was crucial to a commodity aesthetic that relies upon the conspicuous consumption of exquisite objects. The symbolic objectification of social differentiation by asserting a form of consumption from which core middle and lower middle-class fragments have been conspicuously excluded was an important globalizing phenomenon of the 1990s. Excluded in large part by high prices and declining real wages, these fragments also experienced exclusion from the codes governing commodity aesthetics at an historical moment when cultural capital became the calling card of the new middle class.

The second commodity aesthetic also has to do with class symbols and meanings, but in this case the content is about health related to the body and its embodiment in a reconstituted urban "nature." The body and the process of embodiment become associated with self-discipline and control over the body in ways that are analogous to neoliberal ideas about freeing the market from constraints imposed by the state. Living a healthy life in an imagined environment of planted forest, plumbed waterfalls, fountains, and human-designed lakes and ponds became emblematic of an emerging global new middle class. The two commodity aesthetics, one an imagined cosmopolitanism, the other a constituted naturalism of body and environment, were in reality part of a single commodity culture associated with the self-awareness of the new middle class as a globalizing new middle class. The cityscape was being remade in its image and refracted in its feeling of power, privilege, and autonomy. Most luxury housing developers tried to capture the dual commodity aesthetics in their design, promotion, marketing, and advertising. The economy of the globalizing city became dependent on the consumption of luxury commodities of all kinds, including housing.

Variations on Luxury Living

To illustrate and make concrete the connections between changing commodity aesthetics, social values, and living space of the new middle class, we have chosen two housing developments from those with which we are familiar in order to sketch new middle-class abodes. Yuva Sitesi represents variations on planned low-rise, low-density luxury dwellings and Bahçeşehir represents variations on high-rise, high-density luxury apartments along the lines of planned cities within a metropolis. The variations are themes on commodity aesthetics or what the real estate market refers to as "amenities."

Low-rise, Low-density Luxury Living:
Commodity Aesthetics in a Naturalized Environment

Yuva Sitesi helped to set the trend for low-rise luxury housing developments by showing how the two kinds of commodity aesthetics could be combined and trans-muted into changing consumption "needs" of new and upper middle-class house-holds in the 1980s. Yuva Sitesi represents the ultimate in seclusion, security, and privacy in a *naturalized* built environment in proximity to some of the most crowded upper middle-class housing developments in the city and minutes from what may have been *the* premier luxury shopping experience in Istanbul in the 1990s.

Yuva Sitesi is located on the European side north of the city, on hills overlook-ing the Bosphorus. A small development of two or three-story low-rise buildings, it is on a little-traveled road below Ulus Kültür Park and the Bosphorus village of Arnavutköy in an exclusive area known as Portakal Yokuşu. Nestled in a forest with an unobstructed view to the Bosphorus, it affords complete privacy for its owners, who formed a cooperative to pay a developer, who lives on the site, to build it in the 1980s. A high wall along the road with a security force at the gate ensures both security and safety. Yuva is among the most private locations in the city, completely hidden from the dense suburban high-rise developments and congested traffic that passes through Ulus and Levent at the top of the hill on its way to Etiler. The site is most appreciated from the Bosphorus side looking up toward the buildings. Several acres of lawn roll up the slope. Off to one side and partly hidden are the remains of a Byzantine ruin that has been converted into a playground for children. The lawn is itself a place to stroll and enjoy the surroundings. Buildings are earth toned and set back close to the road. Careful landscaping with low bushes and trees separate the apartments from the expanse of lawn. Coming into Yuva from the entrance off the road, there is landscaped parking and more trees that minimize the presence of buildings and parking spaces. Each apartment has two floors, with direct views of the Bosphorus from the second-floor salon and first-floor bedrooms. The two-bedroom apartments are not large, but they are carefully designed with built-in features and dark wood moldings to fit in with the overall design of the building exterior, the grounds, and the surrounding forest cover that surround the develop-ment site. Yuva is secluded, and it is gated, but it is not a gated community. It has neither commercial shops nor services on the premises. Yuva takes advantage of its location to build a naturalized environment on its site, yet has immediate access to commodity cosmopolitanism up the hill on Nispetiye Avenue, where the most luxurious import emporium in the city opened in the mid-1990s.

High-rise, High-density Luxury Living: Cities within Cities

The trend toward living in the city yet apart from it reached its zenith in the mid-1990s. It appeared that those with money preferred the fabricated environment of the *kent*, a city within a city, to the polluted, noisy, congested, overcrowded, and aging city neighborhoods. One example is Bahçeşehir near Halkalı. Turkish for "garden city," this enormous housing project was conceived and undertaken by Emlak Kredi Bank in the mid-1990s. Located on the western edge of the metropolitan area, one enters through a gate into a full-blown conception of a gated city within the metropolis. Built on undulating land, its tens of thousands of inhabits live in various types of housing from ten-story high rises to town houses. The city has a private primary school, a commercial district, and a park that includes a large pond with a kiosk where the "city's" residents and visitors exercise on weekdays and stroll on weekends. Bahçeşehir has its own post office and administrative offices. Bahçeşehir is a short distance from the commuter train line, the major east-west highway, and there even is a special bus that takes residents directly to Taksim in the center of Istanbul. When Bahçeşehir was constructed in the early 1990s, its tall buildings cast dark shadows on the grass of the Trakya plain. By 1997, other housing developments were going up all around it.

Land has been a major form of middle-class accumulation over the entire period from 1950 to the present, but its meaning has shifted from familial and practical accumulation to commodity aesthetic and investment values, emblematic of a shift from welfare state to neoliberal forms of accumulation. Where before property accumulation in forms such as the *arsa* (plot of land) was intrafamilial preservation of a plot or apartment from one generation to another and a source of congealed savings for education, new middle-class families attuned to the global culture ideology of consumption are accumulating property as a commodity aesthetic of the good life and a hedge on risky investments in the booming stock market. On the business side, since 1980 large fortunes have been made in real estate, primarily from a relatively small number of large construction firms and land developers who have accumulated by dispossession. The now-crowded hills surrounding the Bosphorus and around the northern and eastern shores of the Sea of Marmara are alive, but not with the sound of music. Foreign direct investment has entered the real estate sector, pumping up prices that far outpace the prices recognizable by the old middle class. In this way, the new middle class is a part of the global new middle class. Rising expectations of new middle-class households have an effect on the expectations of core and lower middle-class households. What was an upper middle-class apartment a few years ago now does not meet the higher threshold of better locations proximate to highways and beltways. New amenities have been added to the mix of upper middle-class standards for a respectable home, leaving older housing with fewer amenities to a struggling core middle class.

Cosmopolitan Lifestyle and the Global Ideology of Consumer Culture

Neoliberalism created the consumer ideology and led to the capital for transformative change in Istanbul's established upper middle-class culture. It opened up new opportunities for expression and identity in the form of a commodity aesthetic that was visible in housing, shopping, and media representations of the good life, especially through the consumption of foreign goods, entertainment, and travel. New middle-class households led the way in reimagining themselves, with the aid of promotion, marketing, and advertising firms in joint ventures with foreign counterparts, as participants in an emerging global middle class. The 1990s brought new print and electronic media, which opened new channels of communication. In turn, channels to international information of all kinds offered up new images of a neoliberal imaginary for new Istanbul middle-class households eager to shed the material symbols of an identity rooted in post–World War II national developmentalism. The making of a global middle-class culture into its localized variant was not something added to the formation of the middle class; it was a whole new symbolic way of seeing oneself in a new cultural economy. It was always an integral part of the whole process implied in economic globalization and the neoliberal ideology that gave it legitimacy and meaning. What was taking place in Istanbul was also taking place in globalizing cities from Mexico City to Bombay, subject to national and historical specificities.

How did the global imaginary of the middle-class ideal home take on its localized variant in the social imaginary of middle-class households in Istanbul? Öncü turns to media representations. For example, she turns to the medium of television reruns of old Hollywood films along with "slick advertisements featuring gleaming kitchens, antiseptic bathrooms and healthy foods" (Öncü 1997: 61). In Istanbul, 90 percent of households owned color television sets by 1990, but these new imported goods already were being displayed in Istanbul's upscale stores and shopping arcades by the late 1980s

> What captured the imagination of Istanbul's middle classes and became the focus of their desires was the homogeneity of a life-style cleansed of urban clutter—of poverty, of immigrants, of elbowing crowds, dirt, and traffic—a world of safe and antiseptic social spaces where the 'ideal home' signifies clean air, clean water, healthy lives; a homogenous setting and a cultural milieu where adults and children lead active lives, engage in sports, socialize with each other around their barbecue sets in the gardens. (61)

Öncü goes on to describe how this local variant of an invariant global myth about the "ideal home" is marketed to the middle class in the advertisements of big land and housing developers in Istanbul. They all advertise location as "outside Istanbul" but "very close," and can be reached "within minutes" by car on the expressway. They all advertise necessary amenities such as parking for cars, playgrounds for children, and tennis courts, health clubs, swimming pools, and parks for recreation, sports, and healthy bodies. Advertising images and copy that frame these features rely heavily upon the discourse theme of nostalgia for a past Istanbul that has been lost in the polluted present and the promise of a rediscovery of a cleaner, less crowded and congested, less dirty way of life.

By the turn of the twentieth century, the appearance of a new middle class in Istanbul left little doubt that it had become a visible symbolic and cultural hegemon by exerting a disproportionate effect on taste through changing life-style habits of leisure and consumption. Istanbul became a sparkling city full of upscale shopping, international hotels and restaurants, glittering clubs and casinos, new art museums, and scrubbed historical buildings. Two new international airports, sea buses, tramways, and new highways made for smooth connections among different modes of transportation. As the city spread out, so did its transportation improve, increasing rather than reducing the prospect not only of retaining business, social, and personal connections but increasing them.

If lifestyle and work were all there was to the making of a new middle class, we could end our story here. To date, there has been an emphasis on lifestyles and the ideology of consumer culture in the literature. We argue, however, that neither jobs nor lifestyles are sufficient to reproduce a class. From our perspective, families are the key agents in class reproduction, and the most important field of competitive relations for the purpose of reproducing middle-class families is education. In the remaining chapters of the book, we explore how Istanbul new middle-class families struggle to reproduce themselves by means of education.

Notes

1. The double rhetoric of market and democracy went hand in hand in a dominant discourse that was rooted in neoclassical economic thought and Enlightenment political liberty and scientific rationalism.
2. Many aspects of the liberalization period are well documented; see Rodrik 1991; Boratav, et al. 1995, Balkan and Yeldan 1998.
3. Following the military coup of 1980, a new constitution was written and national elections were held in November 1983 to restore civilian government, led by Turgut Özal, who took office on 13 December.
4. Out of total deposits of $4 billion, about half belonged to a little over 1 percent of all deposit holders. The annual average interest income for large depositors was about $7,000 compared to about $150 for small depositors (Zaim 1995).
5. Many middle-class families who sold their houses and gold and deposited the money in time deposit accounts suffered huge losses. For example, a family who sold a house for $20,000 in 1981 and placed the proceeds in a time deposit account could not get even one tenth the value of the same house six years later.
6. There is evidence that wages and salaries were the major contributors to direct taxation. From 1987–90, the effective tax rates on wages and salaries increased from 16.3 to 18.7 percent. During the same period, effective tax rates on profits and other nonwage income increased from 11.9 to 15.9 percent, but the burden in real terms was on the wage and salary earners, shrinking the purchasing power of middle- and working-class households. In addition, reducing expenditures on education, health, and welfare undercut the implied reciprocity between a middle class willing to shoulder the tax burden in exchange for state provision of middle-class welfare in the form of education, health, and housing benefits (Yeldan 1995).
7. Keyder, writing at the close of the 1990s, laments the failure of government to keep pace with the needed investment in infrastructure to sustain Istanbul's leadership in Turkey's global integration. He writes that "a telephone system that was overhauled in the 1980s and was up-to-date at the time has been barely maintained, with no new investment, and is showing the strain. In a city where businesses move frequently, no telephone books were published

between 1987 and 1996; and the 1996 one does not include business addresses or numbers" (1999: 19–20).

8. Keyder (1999: 20) notes that the public phone company that had a monopoly on phone lines also controlled Internet access. Failure to establish sufficient lines slowed communication to the point where large companies set up their own illegal satellite connections. "Pirate" providers offered Internet service to the public.

3

THE MAKING OF AN EDUCATION HIERARCHY

⋗⟨⋉⟩⋌

After the founding of the republic in 1923, among the first acts performed in the Grand National Assembly by the Republican People's Party was the Unification of Education Act in 1924, which placed all types of education under a single authority vested in the Ministry of National Education (*Milli Eğitim Bakanlığı*). Included in this sweep were the existing Islamic schools and the foreign (mostly Christian) schools. The significance of this event is that the founders understood that the republican state would be "realized" and legitimated through a form of "modern" education that was sweeping across Europe from its origins in Prussia and France. The Treaty of Lausanne established the permanent boundaries of the Turkish state. Education played a major role in state formation and, later, in the foundation for creating a national culture and modern economy. Since the Treaty of Sèvres was a part of the Treaty of Versailles, Turkey was recognized as a state in the eyes of the great powers.

What actually constitutes the "modern" is as passionately debated today as it was in the late Ottoman period.[1] Traveling the road of modernity could be invoked by each generation or era and used to judge the degree to which there was a rupture with, or continuity between, present and past. Part of being modern meant constructing a new imaginary of belief in the prospective future that was just over the horizon, a new structure of feeling associated with the word *progress* in the context of a waning empire. Nation-states were empowered to fulfill this destiny within a temporal mode of a generational duration.

In a succinct treatment of the question of what makes modern education "modern," Andy Green provides an answer (1990). From the historical experience of nineteenth-century Europe and America, Green abstracts the common features of a state discourse that viewed an education system as objectively "modern." His formalism resembles the historical practices of social reformers of the late Ottoman and early republican periods who shared a preoccupation with "becoming modern." Green himself qualifies this exercise by noting that modern education had "a long period of historical gestation" and alludes to the uneven development of modern systems as a source of their variety of forms (1990: 1). The evolving state is a key agent of societal transformation. Modern education systems achieve their full potential only as an aspect of nation-state formation. "With the coming of the school system," Green comments, "education became a universal and national concern. . . . Learning became universally equated with formal, systematic schooling, and schooling itself became a fundamental feature of the state" (1990: vii).

Determination of whether an educational system is modern revolves less around the origin of a system than the processes that create it, including the institutionalization of the provision of education, the rationalization of its administration, and the implementation of forms of public finance and control (Green 1990: 2). National education systems are public education systems: they are state financed, state administered, and state controlled. They require education for everyone, licensing and inspection of schools, recruitment, training and certification of teachers, standardization of curricula, and certification of students when they leave school (Green 1990: 2).

To the above characterization we can add the concept of a "system" in the sense of an institution that is unified and hierarchical (Green 1990: 2). Around the globe, modern systems of education are hierarchically organized into primary, secondary, and tertiary levels of schooling. Curricula and certification of both teachers and students are organized around points of exit and attained levels of education. The system is audited and legitimized by the state, which holds positional power over all other institutions and determines the distribution of powers among them. A modern education system has steps, or grades, within each level of the system. This ensures a necessary and sufficient progression from step to step and lower to higher education, including points of exit punctuated by formal certification.

A hierarchical system of attained levels of education is conducive not only to the reproduction of a social hierarchy but also attuned to economic hierarchies related to expertise and manpower needs for a developing division of labor in an emerging industrial economy. Together these features function to satisfy the role that the education system plays in socializing individuals to become loyal citizens and disciplined workers in modern nation-states. Just as the state legitimizes the education hierarchy, the education hierarchy lends legitimacy to the state and other hierarchies—political, economic, social, and cultural. While allowing for significant variation, Green argues that all European nation-states ultimately adopted modern education systems that were then transplanted in other nation-states, reaping the benefits of high rates of attendance, competent teaching, and widespread popular literacy (1990: 3).

The most important education reforms that shaped Turkey's project of becoming modern extended over a century, beginning in the mid-nineteenth century, when the waning Ottoman Empire institutionalized education reforms, slowly shifting power away from the palace to put education, and other institutions, in the hands of an elite group of functionaries. Following the late Ottoman reforms known as *Tanzimat* (1839–76) came the constitutional reforms of the early Republic of Turkey (1923–46). At the end of a century of reforms, republican multiparty political reform and import-substitution economic policies from 1950 to 1980 created the conditions for education reforms aimed at achieving mass universal literacy, universal compulsory elementary education, the introduction of foreign-language instruction in public middle education, and the expansion of higher education opportunities. To this extent, the education hierarchy paralleled a social class hierarchy.

The neoliberal economic reforms that began in 1980 represent a new set of education reforms that, together, institutionalized and legitimated the values and practices of a new middle class.

This chapter traces the state's making of an education hierarchy with special emphasis on the reproduction of the republican elite, which became the upper middle class that transformed itself, along with others, into a new middle-class fragment of the neoliberal state.

Education Reforms of the Early Republican Period, 1923–46

Republican period reforms can be characterized as state experiments in total societal reform under duress of creating a nation-state from the remains of the Ottoman Empire after World War I. Paradoxically, those reforms were prefigured in *Tanzimat*, an extraordinary effort by the Ottomans to reform their own institutions influenced by reforms in Europe. In the last decades of the nineteenth century, Ottoman reformers culled European education institutions considered exemplars that would help shape their own education reforms. The reason why the Turkish national education system today is "modern," in the sense given by Green, is because republican reformers from 1924 to 1946 departed radically from religion and empire to establish a secular nation-state that required secular education reforms.

The education reforms of the early republican period were guided by an ideology of "six arrows" enunciated by Mustafa Kemal Atatürk and his Republican People's Party. The revolutionary plan to create a national culture included the idea of a Turkish citizen, a unified imaginary of the "Turkish" people, their language, and their culture. All these practices were inscribed in the curricula and textbooks of primary and middle schools where the practices of secular nationals were performed daily.[2] In the decades between 1950 and 1975, the system of elite public middle schools emerged to train a core industrial middle class. Andreas Kazamias remarked that:

> Turkish language and literature replaced the previous Ottoman language in 1924, and religion was eliminated; after the 1927 language reform by which the Arabic script was replaced by Latin letters, Arabic and Persian were dropped; the history of Turkey and the Turkish race became the 'pivot' of history courses at all levels of education; pre-Islamic Turkish literature was given more emphasis; and after 1929, the new Turkish Latin alphabet became compulsory as the only medium of writing and instruction. Plans to Turkify the language were inextricably intertwined with the nationalistic policies of the republic; and one of the main purposes of the general high school curriculum has been 'to train a Turk who is committed to the Turkish language, the principles and policies of the Turkish revolution and in general to Turkish ideals' (1965: 132).

In 1921, two years prior to the founding of the republic, Kemal proclaimed that "our national system of education should be something different from the old and something that grows out of our own nation . . . and national genius can only be developed through our national culture" (Kazamias 1965: 115). His famous "Message to Youth" delivered in 1927 exhorted them "ever to preserve and defend the National Independence of the Turkish Republic" (Kazamias 1965: 116). Despite this rhetoric, the paucity of economic and cultural capital limited what could be accomplished. Not unlike Ottoman experience with *Tanzimat*, ideological commitment and bureaucratic-administrative organization did not easily translate into education policies and practices.

Modern education systems serve different masters. The extent to which each is satisfied has much to do with the politics of resource allocation at particular historical moments. Turkey is no exception to this rule. Priorities of the Republican People's Party during the interwar years included the subordination of religious power to secular authority, the suppression of sectarian collective identities in the interest of national unification, and the making of a new social class that would provide political, economic, and cultural leadership. What were the Kemalist education reforms, how did they fit into state priorities, and with what consequences for middle-class formation?

The Kemalist reformers framed their education project as totalizing in scope and revolutionary in intent. They included administrative reorganization, a reconceptualization of schooling, and a change in the content of the curriculum. Most of the important reforms were completed in the early years of the republic and persisted thereafter. The state brought different kinds of schools under a single centralized Ministry of National Education, eliminated the dual system of secular and religious administrations of similar kinds of schools, began graded levels of education, established a system of inspection of schools, certified teachers, credentialed students, and regulated curricula and pedagogy.

The instrument of power was the 1924 Law of Unification of Instruction (*Tevhid-i-Tedrisat Kanunu*) that determined "all education instruments are to be placed under the control of the Ministry of Education" (Kazamias 1965: 118). In this one maneuver, the secular state loosened the grip that religious authority had continued to hold on late-Ottoman education reformers (*Tanzimat*).[3] Ideologically committed, Kemal never really expended the resources necessary to meet the challenges of the 1924 unification of education law. Instead, the final transformation to a modern education hierarchy owed much to the transformation of Turkey into an industrial state based on the accumulation of capital through state ownership of companies and the appearance of an educated new middle class.

The Ministry of National Education oversaw an enormous system of modern discipline and surveillance. With the passage of time, the degree of hierarchical control and regulation of an education system was truly remarkable. Centralized administration extended into the micromanagement of classrooms of the nation. For example, the ministry, in its many branches, makes final decisions about local administrative matters as well as what students will learn, what textbooks will be used, how they will be examined, how teachers will be trained, as well as inspection of schools and evaluation of personnel.[4] The central administration in Ankara is also the agency of education planning for expansion in enrollments and numbers of schools and teachers required. The ministry is known to be monolithic but not single minded in its policies. It does, however, pass down decisions through the press with little or no public debate. An ecumenical Education Council of State (*şura*), composed of high ministry officials, rectors of universities, school principals, teachers and other educators, and persons from business and civil organizations, meets periodically to advise the ministry on a whole range of education reforms that have no particular policy framework or time period for execution. The results of these large national meetings appear in published reports and the press.

Within the ministry are the Directorates of Primary Education, Secondary Education, and Higher Education, as well as myriad other administrative directorates. The ministry in Ankara, the capital of Turkey, appoints teachers and principals; it appropriates money—which is earmarked in the national budget—for buildings, repairs, and equipment; and it has its own inspectors, although the provincial governor also has the right to inspect secondary schools and to report any observed irregularities. The tight bureaucratic control over schools is typified further in the duties and powers of the local school director (*müdür*). The responsibilities of the *müdür* are minutely prescribed by regulations issued by the central office. The director is authorized to inspect classes and the work of the teachers, to see that each teacher provides monthly course outlines, to report to the ministry if the outline is not followed, and to check on homework assignments. The director administers the finances of the school, holds required meetings to inform teachers about matters of school policy, and at the end of the year evaluates teacher performance for purposes of promotion or transfer. All of the foregoing are recorded in writing and sent to the proper directorate in the ministry. Assignment of teachers to schools around the country is centralized in a directorate of the ministry. Kazamias, citing Maynard's earlier unpublished study of schooling, remarked that the comments of principals of foreign schools who had worked in Turkey found government control and regulation of their schools to be stifling (1965: 121).

The Directorate of Secondary Education is of particular relevance to our interest in elite education and its relation to class formation. The directorate oversees all matters concerning middle education (*orta öğretim*), which in 1996 included grades nine through eleven (*lise*, or high school) as well as grades six through eight. The law stipulates that elementary education is mandatory for the first five years of schooling, making the end of fifth grade the first official point of exit from formal education and entry into the work force.[5] The second official point of exit from the system is the end of high school in eleventh grade, at which time students receive a diploma and enter the work force. The third point of exit is at the end of a university education, at which time students receive a degree and enter the work force. There is a fourth tier to the system that confers postgraduate degrees with the title of doctor or equivalent titles.

The major achievement of the early republican education reforms, one that made for a modern national system of schooling, was the different types of schools that had clearly defined functions. The framework was laid out as early as 1913, prior to the founding of the republic, and was chartered in the 1924 Law of Unification of Instruction. Eventually, the cycle of five-year primary schools (*ilkokul*) was universalized and made compulsory. The Ottoman elite high schools (*sultani*) were divided into two cycles. The first cycle of three years was renamed *ortaokul* (middle school) and the second three-year cycle was named *lise* (high school). Together they are referred to as *orta öğretim* (middle education) to distinguish them from lower primary and higher tertiary education.[6] The system is hierarchical, progressive, and normative (a student should move up a grade annually). The exit points conferred recognition of achievement for having attained a level of education that was recognizable to prospective employers. Amid periodic debate, the 5–3-3 progression would remain the standard for decades until the Eight Grade Reform of 1997, when compulsory universal education was extended from five to eight years. During the period under review, middle education included grades six through eleven.

In many countries, the place of vocational and technical middle schools has been met with some ambivalence among middle-class families. Turkey is no exception. Despite the demand for skilled labor in the market and the persistent effort of the Ministry of Education to meet the demands of business for skilled labor, middle-class parents continued to steer clear of this option. Among the most apparent reasons for their reluctance, middle-class families view skilled labor as déclassé because it is closer to physical labor than mental labor. An important structural reason is that the vocational- technical path is an exit strategy, not a step toward higher education that is associated with prestige conferred on university graduates. University degrees symbolized cultural capital that was organizational, managerial, professional, and high technology, all characteristics of being in control and making decisions for a capitalist class or the state. University degrees also credentialed an intellectual elite of writers, scholars, artists, poets, journalists, and other important and influential people who relied on one or another form of cultural capital.

In the waning years of the empire, *Tanzimat* reformers turned to special technical and trade schools in an attempt to encourage students to acquire practical vocational and technical knowledge. But social prestige rested in the *sultani* or sultan's schools, which provided general education and were viewed as the avenue of social mobility into the best bureaucratic positions. A similar attitude prevailed during the early republican period of "nation building" that persists to this day. There was a pressing need to educate lower-level bureaucrats and technicians for more routinized work in business, government, and civil institutions. Republican education policy lent strong encouragement for parents to send their children to vocational-technical schools, but the policy failed. Repeated government attempts over the next several decades also failed to meet expectations.[7] Certification from these schools were viewed by parents as terminal, ending in lower commercial, trade, or technical positions that were less appealing than other occupations more central to the lifestyle of core and upper middle-class families. Past history and the National Education Ministry's own policy conferred on the general *lise* the privileged path to university, promising the most prestigious jobs and the way to a comfortable life.[8]

There are some commonly held ideas about the social hierarchical implications of the general education hierarchy of the republic. As capitalism and a welfare state developed, the industrial class structure also took shape through the division of labor, and education's function in the social division of labor became more important. For unskilled or low-skilled industrial labor, universal literacy was the state's standard. Literacy was slow at first, and only gradually did compulsory primary school become a reality. Even then, the state-mandated rate of completion of five grades, especially in eastern Anatolia and rural areas where the majority of population lived and worked, was low. At first, boys extended their years of primary education, and only after World War II did girls begin to graduate from primary schools. Important occupational categories and social distinctions, based on years of schooling and level of education attainment, emerged and were refined by the ministry. Primary school terminal graduates, for example, shaped the upper fragment of a working class in contrast to middle school terminal graduates, who shaped a lower fragment of a middle class. During the period under review, exit from high school (*lise*) established the credentials of the core fragment of a middle class. The *lise*, in other words, was the standard terminal track for the diploma that conferred the power, privilege, and status of a class above the laboring class.

The different kinds of high schools of the Turkish education system include public high schools; Anadolu schools (*Anadolu Liseleri*), which provide additional skills in a selected foreign language by instructing a certain part of science courses in that language; science high schools,[9] which emphasize science education; vocational high schools, which focus on practical skills; Imam Hatip high schools, which educate imams for performing religious duties at mosques; and private high schools, which have a variety of types to be discussed. In this chapter we will focus on those schools that require Selective Middle School Examinations (SMSEs).

The Beginning of "Selective" Education, 1950–83

After 1950, a confluence of political, economic, demographic, and social trends—slowly at first, then accelerating—increasingly undermined the ability of the general middle school (*genel lise*) to perform its central function of developing a national middle class. A populist concern about an education crisis grew louder and more acrimonious as real education crises coincided with and reinforced political and economic crises at the end of each decade from 1960 to 1980. The main education issues were those of declining quality in public schools, increasingly difficult access to quality public education, and rising aspirations of families for university credentials. This list became a mantra of the core middle-class demand on the state.

When Andreas Kazamias was researching the *genel lise* and its relation to the aspirations of a post–World War II middle class, Anadolu schools had only recently come into being. In 1955, the announcement by the Ministry of National Education that it had established the first five Anadolu schools, adding a sixth early in 1956, coincided with the import substitution policies that ushered in a new phase of Turkey's economic development that would continue for several decades.[10] He took little note of their significance, nor could he have foreseen the implications for middle-class formation after 1980. The Ministry of National Education's intention at the time, however, was clear. Anadolu schools were to be a new type of elite public middle education apart from the existing public *genel lise*.

Anadolu schools came along at a time when Turkey was forging an important alliance with the United States following World War II and during the early decades of the Cold War. Turkey had sent tens of thousands of its own soldiers to fight communist ambitions in Korea while the United States established intelligence operations on Turkey's northern border to listen in on Soviet plans for hegemony over its region. United States Air Force bases were also established in Turkey as a part of its policy of preparedness against perceived Soviet threats. Turkish military commanders and officers formed lasting relations with the highest levels of the Pentagon. A little later, Peace Corps volunteers began to appear in Turkey's new Anadolu schools to teach English and science. The passing of the Fulbright-Hays Act by the United States Congress led to American teachers and researchers coming to Turkey, not to mention dozens of other countries, in increasing numbers. The Ford Foundation gave financial and administrative support to the improvement of Turkish universities, including the construction of the Middle Eastern Technical University in Ankara, today one of a handful of Turkey's prestigious universities and one that teaches subjects in the English language.

Anadolu schools also appeared on the horizon at a time when the government was open to many joint ventures or licensing agreements in manufacturing industries between foreign corporations, many of them American, and fledging Turkish corporations. This was the era when Turkey's class of capitalist industrial families emerged and when large corporate industries began to produce mass consumer goods for the growing Turkish middle class, which was comprised of corporate managers and professionals as well as managers of state enterprises. The unfolding picture was one of stronger Turkish state military, political, economic, social, cultural, and educational ties to America at a time when leftist politics were also ascendant, especially among a generation of Turkish university faculty and students.

The Anadolu schools had far-reaching implications for social differentiation within the middle class. It restored the idea of selectivity that made the *lise* an elite state institution from as far back as the founding of the late Ottoman *sultani*, especially the founding of Galatasaray Lisesi in 1869. A feature that further differentiated the Anadolu schools from their counterpart, the *genel lise*, was a curriculum largely based on foreign-language instruction, particularly in English.[11] Students who were selected entered a preparatory year or two learning a foreign language, with English-language instruction ascendant over French and German languages. This feature of the Anadolu schools consciously and intentionally mimicked education provided by the prestigious private foreign middle schools, but foreign-language instruction also was stimulated by the growing influence of American education and English language as part of American foreign policy in post–World War II Turkey. As America gained power and prestige in Turkey, the Anadolu schools became more attractive and influential among middle-class families who harbored expectations for sending their children to American universities.[12]

The main appeal of Anadolu schools to the core middle class was that they offered foreign-language instruction, almost exclusively in English, analogous to the private foreign schools, but were free of tuition. And by virtue of their selectivity, symbolic capital accrued to those families whose children attended Anadolu schools during a time when general middle schools were entering a period of expansion in number but decline in quality. Ibrahim Emiroğlu (1995), a teacher and school administrator at Izmir-Bornova School when it was included among the first five Anadolu schools, remembers that the Anadolu schools quickly developed a spirit of elitism within the public schools administration. The incremental increase in the number of these schools helped to sustain this spirit over several decades, after which the rapid increase in the number of public middle schools labeled as Anadolu schools came under the suspicion of core middle-class families concerned with their declining quality.

Recall that Kazamias's reason for choosing the *genel lise* as the subject of his research was that it had been widely regarded by officials and ordinary people since *Tanzimat* education reforms of the late Ottoman period as the school for training political, administrative, and economic elites. It also was the school type that symbolized social status and republican privilege. The *genel lise* diploma was the credential that was emblematic of membership in the upper middle class and symbolized a comfortable life. But when Kazamias surveyed parent and student attitudes toward the *genel lise* in 1962, he discovered that the general high school diploma was no longer perceived as a terminal diploma, but rather as a way station along the path to university education. Aspirations of republican elite families had risen in accordance with changes in the economy and society. The education policy of the government of the period democratized education by granting all students with a general high school diploma admission to the universities. This noble aim proved to be premature and short lived.

Increasing middle-class interest in higher education reflected the limitations imposed by the level and conditions of economic development. Istanbul University, founded in 1900, was reorganized in its modern form in 1933. Ankara University and Ege University in Izmir followed suit. There were only three universities until the 1960s, after which the state focused on admitting more students to more universities. Ankara had five major universities and Istanbul four when Boğaziçi University was established in 1973. Three of them taught the curriculum in English. The appearance of these new top-level universities made higher education more of a reality for middle-class families, stimulating even more demand for higher education. The 1980 coup would quell an economic crisis that in part was fuelled by a crisis of quality education that extended across all levels of the education hierarchy.

A political crisis at the end of the 1960s resulted in the introduction of a "selection-out" university entrance examination aimed at reducing the rapidly increasing number of high school students who could expect to attain university education.[13] The effect of the university entrance exam was to turn the general high school diploma into a terminal credential for growing numbers of middle-class aspirants. After 1974, the year of the introduction of the first entrance examination based on a spirit of inclusiveness, the state instead used the exam as a selection-out device that made university education an exclusive, hence elitist, form of education. Less than 10 percent of test-takers scored high enough to enter a university. As the number of annual aspirants steadily increased while the 10 percent result turned into an apparent objective of the state, the state responded by adding new "signpost" universities. Many of those who did manage to pass the entrance examination ended up in institutions that were universities in name only. As for entrance to the handful of prestigious universities, the competition became ferocious. The absolute number of university entrants continued to increase along with the number of new signpost universities, but the state retained its mandate that the top 10 percent of test-takers were eligible to enter university. In the decades under scrutiny, passing the state university entrance exam became the divide between the urban, industrialized upper middle class and the core middle class that grew in numbers but steadily lost ground to the university-educated professional, managerial, administrative, and technical elites that constituted the emerging new middle class.

Elite Education, 1983–2000

The new middle class is envied and admired, but it is never secure. Only three decades into this era of globalization, the economic success of new middle-class families has displaced that of the core middle class that is in decline along with the welfare state that underwrote its privileges, work habits, and lifestyle. The meaning of having a comfortable life has been transformed through the neoliberal cultural ideology of global consumption, stimulated by increasingly sophisticated media and marketing that ratchets up the level of consumption appropriate to new configurations of a comfortable life, all the while maintaining the significance of the idea of a comfortable life as part of a social imaginary. Being new middle class is generally perceived to be a good thing to pursue by those who struggle to attain it.

The Ministry for decades had monitored the annual flow of entrants to universities through a national test initiated in 1974, but was unable to keep pace with growing demand for quality education on all levels of the education system. In 1983, the iconic year that the welfare state was abandoned and the neoliberal state was born, the highly centralized pattern of the Ministry of National Education's gatekeeping took aim at the new middle class by announcing a new national test for admitting the "best" eleven-year-old children to the "best" middle schools. The test is named the Selective Middle Schools Examinations (SMSEs).

In the decades leading up to the announcement of the SMSEs, there was a growing aspiration among middle-class families to provide their children with university education, but this did not necessarily result in a rapidly increasing demand to send them to elite public and private middle schools as a necessary step for entering university. The elite middle schools, especially the private foreign schools, were the places where upper middle-class families sent their children. The tepid attitude among middle-class families changed rapidly as parents felt increasing pressure to seek elite education as a necessity. The 1983 decision of the Ministry reflected pressure to respond to the growing demand for quality education in middle schools and the desire to regulate the emerging competition. After 1983, the number of children taking the SMSEs rose steadily.

In effect, the SMSEs introduced by the ministry created a highly visible, precise, and narrowly defined field of competitive relations for new middle-class families' reproduction by means of selective education. This crucial test was perceived as the roadblock that had to be breached. Parents had to compete to get their children into the best middle schools that offered the highest probability for getting into the best universities—especially university education abroad, the goal of every new middle-class family.

By the beginning of the neoliberal era, middle-class parents were raising their voices about the poor quality of public schools at all levels. The Ministry added new public universities, but their quality was in question at a moment when the emerging new middle class was made up of more entrepreneurial, individualist, and demanding families. Neoliberal ideology was all about economic growth, and growth was all about wealth accumulation and raising expectations for a more comfortable material life. The new middle class was familiar with competitive market conditions of global competition and accumulation of capital.

The demand for privatization of education fit neatly into the neoliberal ideology of privatization and marketization of culture industries in general as well as many other ideas and forms of value that were being converted into commodities for the global market. New middle-class families raised the bar for getting into elite middle schools with their competitive, aggressive approach to winning the SMSEs. New middle-class families also stimulated a demand for new private universities and private schools on all levels of the education hierarchy, from preschool to university. How did this happen? It is in this neoliberal spirit and atmosphere of heightened awareness of the increase in value placed on quality education that the cultural reproduction of the new middle class is played out through the annual state-controlled and regulated SMSEs.

Private Foreign Middle Schools

A small number of private foreign schools that were established prior to founding of the republic (see Introduction) also survived the collapse of the Ottoman Empire. Demand for and reputation of these schools grew along with capitalism, industrialism, and Turkey's modern education system. The neoliberal episode not only would increase the material capital of a new middle class, it also would increase the cultural value of foreign private schools. By the time of our research, parents were demanding more private education at all levels of the education system. When the ministry introduced the SMSEs, along with a selection and preference system that regulated schools' selection of students and parents' preferences for schools, the foreign private schools rapidly ascended to the top of the elite pyramid of Turkey's middle schools. It is ironic that the neoliberal spirit of individualism and entrepreneurship would be expressed through the strengthening of the state's hold on competition for admission to the most desired middle schools. This irony disappears if it is understood that the neoliberal state, through the Ministry, stacked the deck in favor of new middle-class families. We return to this and other related issues in the chapters that follow.

There are several different types of private schools that contribute to the makeup of a complete classification of elite secondary education. As a type, private foreign schools (*özel yabancı okullar*) refers to schools that were founded by foreigners within the present-day boundaries of the Republic of Turkey. With the exception of two, all of the forty-two schools listed by Haydaroğlu (1993) were founded between 1850 and 1900.[14] The period is significant for the growth of foreign education in Turkey. Inside the Ottoman Empire, this was the period of *Tanzimat* education reform and "getting closer to the West." Outside, it was a period during which modern education systems were taking shape in Germany, France, Austria, Italy, England, and America, the major sources of influence on foreign education in Turkey. It was a period during which missionaries and foreign national governments, principally British, French, and American, were very active, not only in the Ottoman Empire but also throughout the Middle East and on other continents. These schools proselytized and offered religious instruction; they also taught natural science, math, foreign language, and aspects of Western culture and history.

Today, only thirteen private foreign high schools remain from the late Ottoman period.[15] Private foreign schools survived the Turkish War of Independence to live on in the Republic of Turkey as a consequence of the outcome of the Treaty of Lausanne. Turkey, in exchange for sovereign borders, agreed to protect the foreign schools within its territory.[16] In the 1920s, Atatürk and the leaders of the ruling Republican People's Party were shaping education policy to fit a secular republic and the problems of nation building. The immediate goal was to circumscribe the influence of foreign schools on a fledgling Turkish nationalism. The thirteen high middle schools that comprise the official category of *özel yabancı okullar* survive from the early republican period.

The private foreign high schools all instruct in their respective foreign languages while also meeting the Ministry's regulations for teaching Turkish language, literature, and history.[17] As a result, they are the most sought-after middle schools in Turkey. Turkey's integration into the expanding global economy after 1980, together with its prospects for joining the European Union, the rise of neoliberal ideology among Turkish political and economic elites (especially in Istanbul), and the growing privatization of education have increased the symbolic and cultural value of private foreign school education over the last several decades. Demand for foreign private schools among upper middle-class families that were determined to succeed in the national private SMSEs came up against the reality of an extremely limited number of places. The ministry constrained enrollments in these schools: in 1995, the total enrollment number for all thirteen schools was 4,384.

Private Turkish Schools

In contrast to policy aimed at private foreign middle schools, the ministry relaxed its policy of constraint on private Turkish schools. The private school sector of the Turkish economy grew as a proportion of the GDP in the 1990s. Among the existing older private Turkish schools, Işık Lisesi was founded in 1885 by the Fevziye Schools Foundation. Darüşşafaka Lisesi was established as the Imperial Orphanage in 1868 and began in 1873 to provide *lise* education through the financial help of the sultan and the khedive of Egypt (Shaw 1976: 111). In addition, there are a rapidly growing number of private Turkish middle schools that instruct in foreign language and compete in the SMSEs. Among them, Koç Lisesi, established by the Vehbi Koç Foundation in 1988, owes its creation to Turkey's most famous industrialist who began his rise to fame after World War II. Most instruct in English, but some emphasize German, French, or another foreign language.

Many private Turkish schools that compete in the SMSEs offer courses in foreign language, but most of them do not instruct in a foreign language. Kalamış Lisesi, founded in 1951, and Kültür Koleji, founded in 1960, are two of the older private Turk *liseleri* in Istanbul, but neither of them match the performance of some schools founded in the 1980s such as Acıbadem Lisesi, Atanur Oğuz Lisesi, Semiha Şakir Lisesi, and Belde Lisesi. The first three were founded in the late 1980s by former Istanbul mayor and school entrepreneur Bedrettin Dalan. The Istek Foundation has established many schools in Istanbul. All private schools in Turkey are regulated through their legal registration as foundations.

A few of the newest private Turkish schools, such as Yüzyıl Işıl, acquired a quick reputation for its elementary school before its middle school was built. Many new private schools, like Yüzyıl Işıl, appeal to new middle-class parents because they offer parents the option of quality education with or without entering children into the SMSEs. The risk for the education entrepreneur is that the school may not be able to do both, and even if it does, it may be punished because the school loses in the all important rank order of "best" schools determined by the state's ranking them solely on the numerical scores of its student test-takers. They do less well as a group than the older established private Turkish schools or new schools that focus on teaching to the test.

Established upper middle-class families had always relied upon a system of elite private middle schools for social and cultural reproduction. There also was a time around the 1950s when some public schools were known for their quality education. By the 1970s, it was apparent to the whole nation that most public schools at all levels of the education hierarchy were unable to maintain their standards. The Anadolu schools were intended to provide the middle class with education comparable to the private schools. This happened only in a minority of the schools. Instead, the privatization of education after 1980 increased the options for new middle-class families at a time when the old core middle class was struggling to find an affordable alternative to the Anadolu schools. Most middle-class families lost ground when it came to material assets in the neoliberal era and were unable to either compete through the SMSEs or place their children in private schools that were safe havens from the decaying public schools. The news was sweet and sour for the neoliberal new middle-class families. They had the money and desire to compete for the state's "best" schools in the SMSEs, but the demand for these schools continued to far outpace the supply despite increasing investment in the private sector of education at all levels.

Notes

1. "Modern" is perhaps the most inclusive keyword in all political and academic discourses related to the past and present of the Republic of Turkey. For this reason, the discourse of "modernism" is also the most contested discourse in Turkish society. Originally associated with "secularism," in the last several decades, Islamic scholars have redesigned its symbolism and claimed the mantle of modernism for themselves. For an interesting and provocative history of the origins of the current revisionism of late Ottoman education, see Fortna 2002.
2. For an insightful account of the early constitution of the nation in the context of the agency of education and the role that the Council for Education Policy continues to play, see Kaplan 2006: 39–64.
3. Other laws, however, placed military schools under the Ministry of Defense and schools begun by other ministries were placed under the joint administration of the appropriate ministry as well as the Ministry of Education.
4. See Kazamias 1965: 118–21. The original organization remained the same, with the addition of other directorates, teams, and groups. For a synoptic view of the ministry's organization, see Baloğlu 1990.
5. In the Turkish education system, middle education (*orta öğretim*) refers to the grades between elementary education (*ilk öğretim*) and higher education (*yüksek öğretim*). These terms refer to levels of an education hierarchy, not to be confused with types of schools. Middle education in Turkey encompasses grades six through eleven.
6. In 1997 the first exit point from the education system was moved from the end of elementary school in fifth grade to the end of lower middle school in eighth grade, in effect raising compulsory comprehensive education from five to eight years.
7. The General Directorate of Higher Education was reorganized in 1927 in an attempt to elevate vocational-technical schooling. Its name changed to the General Directorate of Higher and Vocational Education. In 1933, in yet another attempt to attract students to vocational-technical schools, a new department, the Department of Vocational and Technical Education, was created.

And in 1935, the central ministry assumed financial responsibility for all these schools. See Kazamias 1965: 122.

8. See the section on attained levels of education of the 1958 Grand National Assembly in Frey 1965.

9. These schools were established with the aim of providing education to exceptionally gifted mathematics and science students. They offer a four-year program with a curriculum that emphasizes science and math. The language of instruction is Turkish. Students take the entrance exam for these schools after the eighth grade. There are also some private science high schools that were established in the 1990s. Entry to these private science schools is less competitive.

10. On 23 February 1955, the Grand National Assembly voted to put the cost of conversion of four high schools (*resmi kolejler*) into Anadolu schools, each in a different city, into the education budget. According to a former school administrator and retired teacher who was at public Bornova Anadolu Lisesi when it was converted, the conversions from old *kolejler* to new *liseler* were as follows: from Eskişehir Koleji to Eskişehir Anadolu Lisesi; from Izmir Bornova Koleji to Bornova Anadolu Lisesi (in Izmir); from Kadıköy Maarif Koleji to Kadıköy Anadolu Lisesi (in Istanbul); from Konya Koleji to Konya Anadolu Lisesi. In the same year Samsun Koleji was converted into Samsun Anadolu Lisesi. In 1956, Diyarbakır Koleji was converted into Diyarbakır Lisesi. (Emiroğlu 1995: 18.)

11. Recall that an explicit aim of *Tanzimat* education reform was to introduce foreign-language instruction in order to take advantage of Western forms of administration and military organization for the purpose of improving the Ottoman state.

12. Emiroğlu (1995) associates the Ministry of National Education's decision to teach in English with growing US involvement in Turkish industrialization, the geopolitics of the Cold War, and Turkey's participation in the Korean War. The Anadolu schools would make use of Peace Corps volunteers to teach language and literature during the 1960s and 1970s. Emiroğlu omitted Galatasaray Lisesi, which offers instruction in French, and Istanbul Erkek Lisesi, which offers instruction in German, from his account because they were not part of the original pilot. He acknowledges that both of these old and well-established elite schools were really forerunners of the Anadolu schools and were models for them.

13. The Student Selection Exam (ÖSS, for its Turkish initials) was first applied in the late 1960s. Before that year, each university selected its students via some criteria. However, with the increasing number of youth and the overload of applications, the universities gathered and founded the Higher Education Council (Yüksek Öğretim Kurulu), and a subdivision named Student Selection and Placement Center (ÖSYM, for its Turkish initials). In 1974, the format of the ÖSS exam was changed. In 1980, another big change took place: the number of the exams was increased to two, namely the ÖSS and the Student Placement Exam (ÖYS). A student that did not achieve the specified grade in ÖSS did not have the right to take the ÖYS, and thus, lost the chance to be accepted to a university. This system continued until 1999, the date when the ÖYS was dropped and only the ÖSS was left, with the same format.

14. See Haydaroğlu 1993 for information on the schools and their numbers as follows: nine French Catholic schools, two English schools, four American schools, fourteen Italian schools, one German school, two Austrian schools, two Russian schools, six Iranian schools, and two Bulgarian schools.

15. Kocabaşoğlu (1989) lists the following American schools: İçel Özel Tarsus Amerikan Lisesi, Istanbul Özel Amerikan Robert Lisesi, Istanbul Özel Üsküdar Amerikan Kız Lisesi, and Izmir Amerikan Kız Lisesi; the German school is Istanbul Özel Alman Lisesi; Austrian schools are Istanbul Özel Sankt George Avusturya Kız Lisesi and Istanbul Özel Sankt George Avusturya Lisesi ve Ticaret Okulu; French schools are Istanbul Özel Notre Dame de Sion Fransız Kız Lisesi, Istanbul Özel Saint Benoit Fransız Lisesi, Istanbul Özel Saint Michel Fransız Lisesi, and Istanbul Özel Saint Joseph Fransız Lisesi. Turks began to attend these schools in greater numbers during the 1930s.

16. The Lausanne Treaty also protected Greek, Armenian, and Jewish minority schools, (*azınlık okulları*), religious places, and minority languages. In 1869, as part of *Tanzimat*, France was invited to create a middle school to train diplomats. Galatasaray remains to this day one of

the most prominent schools in Turkey. From the standpoint of education and class issues, Galatasaray Lisesi enjoys a reputation equal to some of the best private foreign schools, but has the price tag and official status of a Turkish public *lise*. This makes it attractive to Istanbul middle-class families that seek its prestige but cannot afford the costs of private foreign schooling. See Vahapoğlu 1992.

17. The schools have adjusted their organization, curriculum, and mission to adapt to periodic education reforms mandated by the Ministry of National Education. During the liberalization period and following the introduction of the state-controlled and regulated Private Middle Schools Examination system, all thirteen schools admitted students to middle schools (grades six, seven, and eight) with the expectation of continuance through high school (grades nine, ten, and eleven). All the schools had "preparation" (*hazırlık*) in the form of one or two years of foreign-language training sandwiched between primary and middle school.

4

FAMILISM

The determining factor in history is, in the final instance,
the production and reproduction of the immediate essentials
of life. On the one side, the production of the means of
existence; on the other side, the production of human beings
themselves. The social organization under which the people
of a particular historical epoch and a particular country live
is determined by both kinds of production.

—Frederick Engels,
The Origin of the Family, Private Property, and the State.

In this period of extraordinary change, such household
structures and extended family values seem to have been less
affected than many other major institutions. They provided an
anchor of relative stability in a sea of changing relationships
and meanings.

—Alan Duben and Cem Behar,
Istanbul Households: Marriage, Family and Fertility.

Reproduction begins on the ground. To paraphrase Engels, the reproduction of human beings and the reproduction of their conditions of existence are the roots of all
forms of economic, social, and cultural practices in human history. What anthro-
pologists understood from the beginning of their discipline is that these practices
are both universal and variable. There is no necessity for households to be formed
by "marriage," but in all human societies, "marriage" of one kind or another is
an important organizing concept for household formation, one of the roots of the
reproduction of our species. Likewise, there is no necessity for marriages to be
formed by a concept of "family," but in all human societies, "family" of one kind
or another is also a root that accompanies marriage formation. And there is no necessity either for marriage or family to be expressed in terms of variable "kinship"
nomenclatures, but every human society has devised a particular kin nomencla-
ture to locate social persons and their relations in terms of marriage and family
relations. Kin terms and relations invariably are inscribed with moral obligations

and appropriate sentiments that establish a regime of expectations, distinctive and separate from all other kinds of coeval social formations in complex societies. The social reproduction of Istanbul new middle-class families is the salient institution for organizing the production and reproduction of this class formation.

The triumph of secular nationalism in a twentieth-century history of republican state reformism frames a logic of Istanbul "familism," by which we mean the expectations, mores, and sentiments that together form a cultural logic that makes sense of enduring practices associated with kinship, family, and marriage. In this chapter, we focus on the logic of familism together with its practices to argue that social capital is a metalogic for practices that, in turn, frame the making of durable social networks. These networks extend beyond the family into other spheres of practice and contribute to the new middle class as a "social" class imbued with its own consciousness and collective interest. These noncapitalist relations of reproduction of a new middle class, intertwined with neoliberal capitalist relations, set the stage for the final chapters of the book, which focus on those practices associated with the most important interest of new middle-class families—namely, their material, social, and cultural reproduction by means of schooling of a certain kind.

An Overview of Turkish Family and Kinship

Alan Duben and Cem Behar place recent Istanbul upper middle-class marriage and household formation in historical context (1991). Their seminal research on Istanbul household and marriage among "literate bureaucratic classes" in the first few decades of the twentieth century suggests that Istanbul marriage and household practices remained stable during a period of rapid change. In retrospective interviews conducted in the 1980s, during the first decade of the transition from welfare state to neoliberal state, Duben and Behar found that the majority of middle-class informants who had married in the 1920s and 1930s stated that theirs were love marriages; the novels of the period give a similar impression. In those heady times of the first decades of the founding of the republic, romantic love was in the air. Nevertheless, we also know from the interviews that although these were labeled as love marriages, they did not involve the radical departure from the family norms that, perhaps, the ideal type required. While the relationship was often initiated by one or both partners, *once they had decided to get married it was necessary to turn the matter over to their families*. The groom-to-be had to ask for the hand of his bride-to-be from her father. And parents might object and use their power and influence to dissuade their children. In any case, whether parental sanction was symbolic or not, *the institution of marriage still ultimately involved the arrangements of two families*. It had not merely become solely a matter of "individual choice" (Duben and Behar 1991: 97). In other words, conjugal privacy, personal emotion (love), and individualism coexisted along with robust shared sentiments, mores, and expectations of the family toward its members.

In mundane Turkish discourse, the word "family" (*aile*) has more than one meaning depending upon its social context. One common use of *aile* refers to the nuclear family of parents and children sharing a residence (*hane*), conflating kin terms and their relationships with coresidence.[1] This is the family codified and certified by the republican state as the official family and corresponds with biological reproduction. Another common use of *aile* refers to bilateral kinship through affinal (marriage) ties. A "big family" (*büyük aile*), from the standpoint of a married couple, consists of her and his parents and their respective families. Kin relations of the same generation extend outward to families of brothers and sisters, and from different generations upward through families of fathers and mothers to grandparents. Beyond three generations, kin terms are derived from the generation below and become few. Genealogical memory weakens beyond the third generation.

Kin terms retain a distinction between paternal and maternal relatives. From the perspective of a conjugal couple, husband and wife each retain control over their own consanguineal lines of sentimental, social, and material support. As individuals, husbands and wives have parallel sets of reciprocal obligations toward each member of their kin group.

The sentiments and obligations implicit in the big family constitute a social contract that underwrites the use of kin networks to extend the social mores of kinship to mutual support in solving a wide range of problems related to provisioning in every sphere of civil, bureaucratic, and market competition. Familism, in the context of building social networks, extends the morality of kinship into spheres of bureaucracy and market. A reciprocity of favors as well as other benefits relies upon reciprocal—and often implicit—meanings and moral understandings about the value of social relations in and of themselves as activities associated with practices of accumulating social capital, which justifies the view that the middle class is a social class with its own ways of reproducing itself.

Social Capital

There are many definitions of social capital. Controversy among experts over the meaning and use of this concept for analyzing social issues related to accumulation of capital has resulted in debate that has been inconclusive. In this section, we explore social capital by its *function*. One function is the contribution of social capital to the reproduction of the new middle-class family. In a recent edited volume on the concept of social capital, the editors settle on the following definition and its use: "Social capital—broadly, social networks, the reciprocities that arise from them, and the value of these for achieving mutual goals—has become an influential concept in debating and understanding the modern world" (Schuller, Baron, and Field 2001: 1). The second function of social capital is its contribution to creating human capital, conceived as a bundle of qualities embodied in the person or individual.

Anthropology is a field that has a long tradition of exploring forms of reciprocity and their correlations with spheres of exchange, different social institutions, and related issues of economic organization such as commensuration of value among different spheres of exchange. The main point is that the creation of value is embedded in various social institutions, particularly those of family, marriage, and kinship. In chapter 1, we cited Bourdieu's concept of multiple capitals as a way to think about class reproduction in complex societies. In addition to economic and cultural capital, he defines social capital as "the aggregate of the actual or potential resources which are linked to possession of a durable network of more or less institutionalized relationships of mutual acquaintance and recognition [that] provides each of its members with the backing of collectively-owned capital as actual and potential credit" (1997: 46–58). With regard to Bourdieu's institutionalization of the forms of capital, economic capital is institutionalized as "property rights," cultural capital as "education qualifications," and social capital as "durable networks."

Bourdieu's argument is that in a capitalist society, all the forms of capital are subordinated to serving the goal of the capitalist mode of production, which would be the pursuit of profit. Therefore forms of exchange that appear outside the capitalist sphere are actually disguised forms that serve capitalist accumulation. Perhaps. But he goes on to say that cultural and social capitals are "never entirely reducible" to economic capital (Bourdieu 1997: 54). The reason he gives is that social and cultural capitals have their own respective "efficacies." This weak line of reasoning nevertheless opens the door for "familism" to compete with abstract "economism." There is recognition of the reality of the operation of multiple meanings of capital, operating in separate but overlapping spheres of exchange of different kinds of values within a dominant capitalist system of value.

Social capital is a way of accumulating value that avoids the money cost and risk associated with the capitalist market in all its forms, production to consumption. But first and often foremost, it is a form of sociability governed by the morality of familism extended and modified to fit other noncapitalist forms of value creation. Above all, the highest moral value must be that of security, trust, honor, and commitment to others because they commit to you. These values survive across generations and have the capacity to grow. Corporations, in contrast, increasingly reveal their true value, which consists of the time-dishonored view of selling to the highest money bidder, and in reducing obligations of every kind to their workers who exist only as abstract labor.

The recent increase in all forms of social capital around the world as evident in the World Social Forum, and hence, the recent increase in attention paid by social analysts to the concept of social capital, emanates from the success global corporations have experienced in cutting the ties that bind and commit, evident in the World Trade Organization. Among those ties are their obligations to nation-states and families, increasing interest in all forms of social networks and the value of social capital around the globe.

Making a Marriage and Household

The following two narratives were written by a narrator when she was asked to tell stories about family obligations and how families help each other. She chose to narrate stories about her own big family. At certain moments, the narrator interrupts her narrative to comment on practices or sentiments. These comments are bracketed in the text.

Narrative: A Suitable Partner: Leyla's Introduction to Ahmet

Leyla had completed her education in the US and returned to Istanbul. She was twenty-eight years old. She was ready to get married and her parents were also anxious to get her wed. [Turkish upper middle-class families would like to see their children get settled and have a family after they complete their education and find a job. They think that getting married is especially important for girls because then they will have some protection and not be alone in the future. Middle-class families want their daughters to be educated and to have careers, but this should not come at the expense of having families. Marriage is still important. Young women who get college degrees and start work life get married between the ages of twenty-four and twenty-eight. Leyla was at the upper limit when she went back to Turkey. However, she had been abroad for years, so that establishing a circle of friends at the workplace where she might meet a prospective husband would take time.]

At that point, Leyla's maternal uncle Orhan's business partner Cemil had a recently wed daughter Defne. Defne had gotten married to an economist and small business owner Baran a few years ago. Her marriage was also intermediated by a friend. Defne, who knew and liked Leyla from their summer complex [both Leyla's and Defne's families had summer houses in the same complex] thought that Baran's brother Ahmet would be a good match for Leyla. He was about the same age, educated, and a decent person. Ahmet was a chemical engineer and he was a partner with his brother Baran in the same business, manufacturing shampoos and soaps for hotels. Defne asked Leyla if she would be interested in meeting Ahmet. Leyla assented to the meeting. They met and liked each other, and afterward they started going out to get to know each other better. Leyla's parents knew about the situation and approved of it because they wanted their daughter to find a suitable partner, and they had heard from Defne's parents that Ahmet was a nice young man. In the end, Leyla and Ahmet decided to get married and everyone was pleased.

[Matchmaking efforts are pretty common and well accepted in middle-class Istanbul circles. Married and nonworking women socialize with their friends once or twice every week at tea parties or card parties. These get-togethers create strong social networks for women that function in parallel to men's networks. During these parties, women talk about all kinds of issues, family problems and daily hurdles, and seek help and advice from each other. There might be competition and sometimes tensions among them, but they still stick together and support each other. There is a lot of conversation about young people who have reached the age of marriage. These older women who might have known these young people since they were children or who are close friends with their parents become pretty good judges at evaluating who would be a good match for whom. And they do the matching/intermediation willingly.]

The making of Leyla's marriage involved no less than three big families and included two important business links. Marriage is both a family and individual affair. In Istanbul, it is not uncommon for marriageable-age persons to find each other independently of their families, but these situations may constitute the strongest case for familism, not individualism. Delaying marriage until completion of university education and finding a job are expected. Starting a career takes time and money. Most marriages do not presume that the married couple will live with one or the other's parents, but it does presume that the families have an interest in a foundation built on education and employment as preconditions for marriage. Sentimental attachments and material interests combine to make good marriages.

The expected and most common pattern is for families of the prospective husband and wife to contribute to setting up a separate household. The expectation is that the prospective husband's side will provide the furnishings for the living areas of the domicile and the prospective wife's side will furnish bedrooms and kitchen. A child is expected within a year or two, so there must be available resources for childcare and domestic services. In the case described above, Leyla's father had planned for his family years in advance by investing in a small apartment building. His children, Leyla and her brother Haluk, were expected to move into separate apartments in the same building upon marriage. This expectation was fulfilled, establishing a situation that was the facsimile of the living arrangements of a patriarchal household-family. It is not uncommon for upper-class and upper middle-class families who have the resources and situation to make such living arrangements, but the strong trend is for new middle-class marriages to create new households, often in separate parts of the city. Spatial separation is an important topic of conversation between the two generations of relatives, but it should not be read as social distancing, though that might be one reason in particular cases. To a remarkable degree, Turkish families, across generations, are in constant, often daily, contact by telecommunication but also by getting together weekly or biweekly for sociability and commensality. Food is important in Turkish culture and plays a central role in keeping members of the big family informed about everyone's activities, problems, and successes. Parents remain involved in their children's families, more so when the latter have children, and support them wherever necessary, but do not interfere in the practical and mundane matters of the household.

The sentiments associated with kinship mores and kin terminology are extended also to friends or associates. One of the strongest arguments for the reproduction of a social class by means of the reproduction of families is the very common practice of matchmaking. Matchmaking is a transaction of high social value that brings separate families together through friendship on the assumption of establishing durable (lifetime) relations. Many upper middle-class women with education are not employed. They form associations through neighbors, friends, and associations other than employment in the market. Men are sometimes involved when they are the source for locating a prospect, but making matches, as indicated above, is mostly a women's field of activity that remains within a sphere of social value. Making matches includes assessment of a wide range of specific values, from beauty and handsomeness embodied in the prospective partners to the material worth of whole families. Matchmaking, as the above narrative suggests, brings a relationship of two people "out in the open," into a social setting where valuation consists of qualities that are assessed by a number of people. As a standardized form of reproducing marriage, the collective result is a marriage market of a limited kind. It is a market for partners that is aimed directly at matching social class using criteria of education, wealth, income, occupation, family background, reputation (expressed in the phrase "coming from a good family") and a host of characteristics such as traits that suggest compatibility of personality and disposition. Caring for each other and love (*sevgi*) are high on the prospective couple's list, as are other qualities that parents assess in their own interest.

When Rutz talked informally with Boğaziçi University students, young women with boyfriends they had found on their own offered the comment that they would never marry anyone to whom their parents objected. Many of these students were expecting to go abroad for further education. When Rutz asked these women whether they would live abroad, many of them expressed concern about missing their parents, especially young women who would miss their brothers. Brothers tend to be involved in their sister's welfare throughout adult life and often express their duty as protecting their sister. Young women express particular concern about the welfare of their mothers, but also their fathers. Older brothers are expected to watch over the welfare of their younger brothers. These are lifelong commitments.

Young men were more willing to go abroad for postgraduate education and to entertain the prospect of living abroad. Most of these university students were sure they would marry a Turk. This expression of assurance stemmed from the sentiment that it would be difficult for a non-Turk to fit into a Turkish family. Notwithstanding these sentiments, it is not unusual in the new middle class for marriage partners to be from different countries. These and other sentiments are consonant with the expectations of the cultural logic of Turkish familism. At the same time, they allow for individuals to find each other as persons and to assert a degree of independence in ways that pay respect to all those who have a stake in their lives. Some parents of these university students worry about their children going abroad and finding a spouse. They confided in Rutz that they hoped their child would marry a Turk. Their nervousness emanated from common hearsay about divorce, separation of the married couple from their families, and the prospect of socializing the alien spouse into the mores and expectations that were implicit in their children's upbringing, including the desire to have their children live in Istanbul and to enjoy the privileges of being grandparents. Aging is an issue in a society that is just beginning to experience placing parents in nonfamilial retirement institutions. Parents are constantly on the lookout for ways to help their adult children. There is an implicit understanding that children have responsibilities toward their parents that include taking care of them in their old age. The issue has more to do with social mores than material welfare.

The 1993 Survey, conducted at an early stage of our research, was designed to locate economic, social, and cultural indicators that distinguish one class from another. One indicator was matching attained levels of education of household heads and their spouses. Males were almost always designated as the head of household. In our survey sample of 242 upper middle-class households, in which the male head of household had a university degree or higher, over half the wives matched the same level of education attainment (59 percent, 132/242). When we included the number of wives that had attained a high school diploma by completing eleventh grade (91), the ratio jumped to 92 percent (223/242). It is rare for the wife of an upper middle-class household to have a higher attained level of education than her husband. These results support the tentative claim that education is an important value in marriage matching.

Upper middle-class families also are concerned with the quality of education. Additional support for this conclusion comes from our data on the types of schools that are of value in making marriage matches. In 44 percent of households (52/117) where the male head of household had an education in a private foreign-language school, Anadolu school, private Turkish school, or education abroad, spouses were educated in the same school types. The number of these schools as a proportion of all schools is very small.

In the 1993 Survey, we looked at occupations of 258 upper middle-class household heads and their spouses categorized as managers, businessmen and women, engineers, academics, professionals, and service providers. The most important finding was that 63 percent of wives had no occupation even though many of them had higher education credentials. This finding from a nonrandom sample is consistent with the frequently heard comment that one of the privileges of being upper middle class is the luxury of having a spouse at home for the family. According to the Turkish Civil Code, the husband must give permission for his wife to work outside the home. Unmarried women university students interviewed by Rutz complained that some prospective employers did not take them seriously and disdainfully sent them home. Be that as it may, women who are in the daily workplace work together with men without gender segregation.

The above sentiments and expectations speak to the solidarity of families for themselves and also in relation to others of the same class through marriages. The divorce rate in Turkey is reputed to be as low as 2 percent, but we know nothing about the rate among new middle-class families. From the perspective of a logic of familism, when people meet or hear about single men and women who do not marry, they express some surprise. Single young men seeking apartments are sometimes looked upon with suspicion, and single women who live alone seem to be contrary to the commonly held belief that women need male protection. None of this seems to affect the ultimate acceptance of unmarried adults, both men and women, by their families. To the contrary, unmarried adults without the responsibilities of their own household-family often contribute even more to their "big family."

The following narrative illustrates the depth of ties that bind one generation to another as expressed in a father's actions toward a daughter when things go wrong. Familism can function as a hedge on wrong decisions or risky ventures. It can also lead to flexibility in resource allocation. One aspect of this familism is the mobility of kin in their residential patterns. It is common for a relative to move in or out of an apartment according to the needs of other kin. This openness to circulation of persons among places contributes to tighter bonds of kinship that reinforce the big family in an urban setting where the high cost of real estate and apartment size would atomize social space. It also contributes to a kin-ordered division of labor and allocation of residential space that can accommodate many situations over different periods of time. Rather than an inconvenience, moving about often is viewed as an opportunity to reinforce sentiments, reinvigorate households, and keep others informed about goings on. The latter include all the serious issues that relate to family affairs and problems. These particular bonds of kinship may extend beyond kin to include friends of kin.

Narrative: Accommodations: Taking Responsibility

[It is very common for daughters to go back to their parents' home and live with them again after divorce. In fact, that is still the norm despite the fact that some divorced working women set up their own apartments. Parents take in their daughters willingly in most situations. Daughters tend to be very close to their families and they keep up their close relationship with their parents even after marriage. Therefore they do not hesitate to go back to their parents' home.] I went back and lived with my mother and later with my older brother Mustafa's family for years before I remarried. I worked while I was getting my PhD, but my family supported me in many ways. Mustafa's daughter Deniz and her daughter went back and lived with Deniz's parents for years. Mustafa took over all of his granddaughter's responsibilities and education expenses. Deniz started working with her father in his business. They lived together until Deniz's daughter became a teenager and the apartment where Mustafa's family lived became too small to accommodate them all. Even then, Mustafa and his wife Belma rented an apartment close by for Deniz and their granddaughter and redecorated it, always taking on the expenses for such situations. Faruk's wife Dilek went back to her family after her divorce and even lived with her aunt (mother's sister or *teyze*) for a while because her parents lived in Izmir [a large city several hours from Istanbul.] Her aunt gladly accommodated Dilek and her daughter in her apartment. Dilek now lives with her mother and daughter in another apartment in Istanbul. Her father has passed away and her mother lives with her.

Familism, Social Networks, and Reciprocity

Social networks, many of them based on the reciprocity of favors, morph into friendship networks, schoolmate networks, neighborhood networks, and so on through the different spheres of social transactions that solve problems of marriage, employment, health, legal matters, housing, bureaucracy, and education for members of the new middle class. These networks do not just happen; they are actively pursued, nourished whenever possible, and are the first recourse to solving mundane or more important problems.

From the point of view of credentials, careers, and business, there is no clear boundary between upper middle-class and new middle-class families. What they have in common is control over and access to the possession of certain positional goods, especially higher education degrees as credentials, and expert knowledge in areas of the new economy. Expertise as a positional good distributed in various sectors of the political economy, both public and private, characterizes the material boundaries of the field of competitive relations for new middle-class families to reproduce themselves. Access to this fund of expertise through official bureaucratic or administrative channels is circumvented by the creation of social networks that operate on principles of the reciprocity of favors that can vary by context.

The cultural ideology of familism is the basis for constituting a general reciprocity that is based on the mores of members within the big family that are extended to non-kin such as neighbors (and their kin), close friends (*dostlar*) and their friends and kin, classmates and their classmates and kin, and friends, and so on. Social networks do the work of governmentality, in a general sense, by the logic of reciprocity of favors.

The logic of social reciprocity operates across the whole field of competitive relations governed by the cultural ideology of familism and the reciprocity of favors. From the point of view of persons within such networks, the logic of reciprocity of favors requires the work of constantly extending a social network to accumulate diverse connections that are constitutive of a stock of potential favors necessary to solve the problems that arise in Istanbul everyday life. The networks of reciprocity of favors among near-equals in terms of social class can ultimately penetrate the norms and boundaries imposed by formal civil, legal, political, and economic organizations.[2]

The cultural ideology of familism is one of selfless mutual aid in times of need, irrespective of the context of the receiver, the impact on the giver, and the context of the request. "Help" is freely offered within the big family. Sahlins (1965) has referred to this mode as "balanced reciprocity." There is no immediate return expected; indeed, the kind of return, its duration, and even who will be reciprocated is underdetermined. In a series of permutations of expectations and sentiments governing reciprocity of favors, there is a movement from a sphere of family to a sphere of big family, and from there to successive spheres of extended kin, friends, classmates, and contacts in the spheres of bureaucracy and business. The image is linear and from a single point of view, but the reality is intersecting planes that must be imagined from multiperspective positions. The main point is that favors, often indirectly through third or fourth parties, are reciprocated and that there are many contextualized understandings of what is being reciprocated and by whom. Understandings are often implicit and unstipulated, leaving room for interpretation of contexts, further enhancing the prospects of unknown future outcomes. General reciprocity relies on strong, often implicit social mores and intergenerational connections. Families that meet these conditions provide the best prospect for social reproduction.

General reciprocity is embodied; it has a face, a memory, and a history. But from this ideal point in a cultural logic of reciprocity of favors, there are fine gradations of kind and duration based on social distance and its relation to the norm of reciprocity that involves both implicit and explicit expectations. The implicit norm, depending on relation and context, weakens, until at the outer extension of series of linked favors across boundaries such as family, big family, friend, classmate, neighbor, etc., the logic of reciprocal favors arrives at a quid pro quo exchange that suggests social distance, a weakening of social mores, and an inability to extend reciprocity beyond a very limited duration. Social distance and time are the most important parameters. The more indirect the social connection, the more likely the favors are to be explicit, consciously acknowledged, and concluded in stipulations of the return favor and its temporality.

The temporal duration between reciprocation is irrelevant where the ideology of familism is most active, for example, within the family or among close friends, but a favor gained through numerous links to solve an immediate problem that would result in a short duration of reciprocation, especially if it were defined by the parties as a single nonrecurring problem within a unique context, falls at the outermost border of a system of reciprocal favors. "Negative reciprocity" is Sahlins's phrase for what comes close to being capitalist logic in which the explicit intention of each party is to maximize the gain from the other within an amoral framework of possessive individualism (1965). Social mores become detached from a process of accumulation. Commensuration, the ability to measure all values across different spheres of exchange, is taken for granted as the natural social order of things and persons.

Lomnitz, in her analysis of the reciprocity of favors among urban middle-class Chileans in 1971, described a system of reciprocity of favors in an environment of scarcities: of quality jobs, of money (borrowing from banks was beyond reach), of schools. Most urban middle-class Chileans worked for the government. The system of reciprocal favors emerged in the context of class-oriented political patronage, where political favors among equals served the middle class better than political party loyalties. Her description of the condition of a new middle class at that time bears some similarity to the Turkish urban middle class of the same period and at a similar stage of economic and political development, when most middle-class jobs were to be found in state enterprises and the state had created the modern family beholden to its policies. Accumulation by dispossession discussed in chapter 2 would not have happened without a system of reciprocity of favors between entrepreneurs and the bureaucracy.

Social Capital in the Creation of Human Capital

Coleman observes that "there is one effect of social capital that is especially important: its effect on the creation of human capital in the next generation" (1988: 104). The chapters that follow focus on the cultural reproduction of Istanbul new middle-class families in the context of the high value these families place on getting their children into the most selective middle schools. To succeed, their eleven-year-old children must score high enough on special national examinations that require intensive planning and preparation, often over several years. In the Introduction to this book, we describe what happens on test day. The test is so serious that it involves the lives of all the family members, but especially the daily life of the mother that can extend over a period of years. A few words from a tutor summarize all the comments in our interviews devoted to the investment of the mother in her child:

> My understanding is that mothers are more into this work than fathers. But some fathers also lend a hand. There seldom are many. But many more mothers; mothers exert more effort. . . . The mother is an important part of the family. The mother is very, very important. It's not necessary to develop the brain of the child. It [the Selective Middle Schools Examination] is about strengthening memory. At home, when at the table eating, it's the mother repeating. In the toilet, in the bathroom when washing, you say to the child, "What is that date?" Seriously, the mother is working this way with a very strict dialog and it is impossible to succeed without this. My wife tells me that mothers say, "It is like our second spouse. Every night this exam is our thing, in our meal, our subject matter." It's the time of the fifth grade. It's very serious for families. Generally, the family studies plenty. Families are very affected by this work. That year is cut. Truly, it is very difficult to make these affairs work because of the way we live with two children, our relatives and closest friends. We aren't inside their house, but we feel it. They are explaining this continually.

A part of the social capital in the tutor's comment concerns the mother's preparation of the child's habitus. A child, parents say, will want to play, to be with her or his friends, to watch television or play computer games. It is not the things in themselves that are the problem; it is the dispositions of an eleven-year-old habitus. In Turkey, as in most places, the child is beginning to experience a freedom to play away from the family and among friends. The Istanbul middle-class family is a social family. If friends and relatives do not visit weekly, it is because the family members are visiting them. During the year of the examinations, sociality and commensality cease.

The mother begins to reprogram the child. Social capital in this context is between individuals. Mothers who succeed are said to "calm" the child. The dispositions of the child are slowly transposed into the discipline of the test. The social capital of the mother, in the form of her own ability to gain the "trust" of the child, is key. Fathers are often jealous when their wives begin to focus on the tasks ahead. Determination to win is the driving force of the mother, in turn often driving her husband to express his hatred for the test and cursing the state. Empathy helps the mother to bond with the child, a moment when the child is more attached to the mother than to his or her play. Our interviews with parents about test preparation of their children reveal a gendered discourse composed of the above themes.

When test preparation begins in earnest, it consists of overloads of homework from schools, weekly visits to tutors who drill the child with endless test questions and mock tests, and more visits to lesson schools that teach test subjects. Invariably, it is the mother who participates fully in all these activities. The tutor in the above excerpt alludes to mothers being managers of the whole operation. Our interviews with parents lend strong support to this claim.

The most important creation of human capital in the child is revealed in a quip many husbands make about their wives: "my wife is taking the test with our child." The following excerpt from a working mother is neither an exaggeration nor is it uncommon:

> I started going on Saturdays and Sundays. . . . Bilge is someone who respects all of my efforts. She graduated from the German school and is someone who believes in a core education. She said, "I'm really curious about this Erkan [the tutor]. Who is he? I want to see it for myself, and I won't be convinced by what you tell me unless I go there and see it. So when she came to Istanbul for two or three days we went together to Erkan's on a Saturday. The session started at 8:30 and we sat there. I mean, from 8:30 AM to 1:00 PM. It's not a short time. I took notes for two hours and Bilge took notes for two hours and then she said to me, "This is tough. I've taken a lot of notes, I've studied at Harvard at Wharton, I can write really fast and can follow the class while I'm taking notes but I could almost barely do this."

The human capital of the child, as measured by his difficulties with speed and accuracy in answers to the tutor's test questions is augmented by the social capital of his family. Not only does his working mother improve his scores by preparing along with him, a friend gets involved and, in addition, another member of the family works with him on the child's math test questions. Participation of the parents in their child's education can raise her or his performance and add to human capital, qualities or skills that inhere in the person.

Sentiments of Working Parents

Hasan and Nuran both work. He works as a manager for a textile company that is engaged in export trade. She is a university teacher. Their son Can, eleven years old, attends a private school. Wary of registering Can in the private SMSE, and unfamiliar with its rules and procedures, they nevertheless bow to social pressure and enter Can in the tests. In the narratives, Hasan and Nuran talk about the stress, sacrifice, and frustration they encounter in an attempt to fulfill their obligation as parents to provide their son with quality education. The first big step is winning the private SMSE.

Abbreviations: Hasan (H); Nuran (N)

H: When I consider the emotional side to it, there is a terrible crush. People are in this thing, stepping on each other. I mean, number one [in the annual SMSE] comes out with a score of 100. It is out of a hundred and you have to get in this group and you have to move up here. Let me tell you about our sacrifices and Nuran will fill in what I forgot.

   The program that is carried out in this test preparation is focused totally on Can, I mean, a kid-oriented program is made. I arranged my work strictly according to Can. In the firm, everybody knows that after 5 PM, Hasan cannot be called to a meeting or Hasan won't come to a meeting on Saturday. Why? There's Can. I mean, the firm could accept this. They think, "We will work with this man after he is done with this."

If Nuran stayed in Istanbul, she could not give herself to her job in Antalya [a province in southern Turkey a day's ride from Istanbul by bus or an hour's ride in an airplane, with hours of waiting at both ends of her trip]. She stays at the university for three days and comes back because we thought this routine would make Can feel her absence less. I mean, here, as we see in all other families, the family devotes itself to the kid. If I think about the big family, my father, mother, brother . . . All of them try to make Can happy. How can they help Can. . . . And here my brother can even help in teaching him. He studies certain subjects with him because he is closer to those and he likes them better.

There is an extreme example that comes to mind here, one that I heard on television. A woman quits her job when she was in the position of a vice executive officer because her daughter will take the SMSE that year. It is not a leave of absence; she even loses that opportunity. And in order to feel the same things with her daughter she goes on to get a master's degree at Koç University. They start studying together for her to be able to communicate in the same frequency, to be able to support and direct her program. There are people [pause], families, who change their lives so much.

N: It is the same for me. The administrators let me come to Istanbul from the university at Antalya; I mean, they are more tolerant. My weekly routine is to stay there for three days and come back here. Plus we do not watch television . . . because the test is very important. We don't have family visits. We don't have any family or friend visits, zero. I did not see my mother at all. My family does not come here either. We do not accept visitors. I mean, really, we could not see any of our friends in these two years and we cannot go. New year and other holidays are included in this. There is no social activity.

After Hasan and I take Can to lesson school (*dershane*), we sit in Bebek Kahvesi [a coffee house in the Bosphorus village of Bebek] and then we take him back home. Only five minutes alone together, a time limited to Can's schedule. Isn't the social hierarchy inverted? What has the state done? Other than that, everything, shopping, other needs, are arranged according to Can. But let me tell you that we really got bored of this life. We are waiting patiently for this year to pass. I mean, it became a whole way of life and became very boring. But of course, we do not reveal this to the kid.

Sentiments of a Besieged Working Father and Managing Mother

Ferda and Yavuz live with their daughter and son Erkin in a beautifully decorated and spacious apartment in the hills above Fenerbahçe. Yavuz, a member of a family of hoteliers, has a decorating business. Ferda was preparing Erkin for taking the private SMSE in the spring.

Abbreviations: Ferda (F); Yavuz (Y)

F: In Turkey, education is very limited, only some schools give future-oriented, very good education where foreign language is in more established conditions. Plus to guarantee his future, my son wants to get his education abroad. In any case, there are only two or three schools to provide this. He says that if he enters a private middle school, he will have this privilege. I supported Erkin. The goal is to be able to reach the best education condition in Turkey. I think like this.

    Now he goes to school at noon, comes back at 5 pm. Mornings, around nine, we start to study until eleven-thirty at home by ourselves. Mondays from eight to noon we go to two private tutors. Wednesdays and Fridays [from eight to noon] we go to lesson school (*dershane*). Tuesdays and Thursdays are the same as Saturday and Sunday: Erkin and I study intensively. Sometimes, there are days I don't send him to school because the private tutor has some test exams on Mondays. To be prepared for those exams, to be able to close the gap on fourth grade, we do some tricks like that.

F: If you ask, "When is play time?" it is after studying two hours when he has a break. He can only play at that time. In addition, on weekend nights there is no study. Otherwise, he is always studying.

Y: When we look at the moral side [of test preparation], my wife became so involved with the competition, the test, that over one year she bonded with the kid, I mean, in one and a half years our family order has been changed. In plain language, our relationship in bed almost came to an end; because of this stressful environment, this is so strange, they [Yavuz's wife and son] are so motivated. For example, coming home with a 78.4 score, asking questions like which questions do they answer, why it happened that way, searching for answers, looking at books, asking somebody else. They are working day and night. And in the evenings, my wife turns to me with eggplant colored eyes, half open eyelids, and as soon as possible being parallel to the ground resting her body, there is nothing left after the [day's] effort. She doesn't have anything left for me. Where has our social life gone? We have nothing. We have a membership to Cine 5 [cable TV]. Thank Allah. By paying an extra fee, we can watch some movies. Other than that, I mean, in terms of social life we are in a heartbreaking condition. I used to be in favor of going out a lot, very friendly, being channeled to kids totally. Ferda is managing my life totally, like I'm in a vegetative state.

Y: Erkin lives with a heavy pace and without playtime, besides play is not physical, only mental games on the computer. [Erkin's dream is to be a computer engineer and Ferda has promised him his dream.] What is Erkin doing? Turns on his computer, putting in whatever it is, plays three games or sits down and plays with k'nex doing whatever. Again there is no physical activity. However, at his age a kid should have a lot of physical activity—still, my son, even though we have an area over the garage downstairs to build a place for basketball, there is no move toward taking the ball and throwing it into the basket. I mean there is no action. Zero action. The only thing he does is with the bike I got for him last summer. He rides the bike at the summer house, plays a little ball, and swims in the sea. No other movement. But other than that, at the summer house, too, summer passed with studying. I believe in that too, I mean. Our summerhouse is in Avşa on the sea. Once a week we came here [Istanbul] by sea bus to get private lessons and went back next day, repeating this routine. By doing that kind of crazy thing, I mean.

F: Now, here we shouldn't relate this lack of physical activity only to the tests. I mean, of course, there is a study schedule. Okay, we are doing some juggling for not to lose time, but in Istanbul like playing basketball, being in sports, going swimming, all these have a large bill anyway. I mean, to do these somebody should be assigned with a car and take the kid from one place to another on weekends, waiting for him and taking him back. To me, another reason for choosing private schools is that. They have very nice organized sports. I mean kids in every way live in perfect conditions. It's never like in America. The child goes to his school at elementary, the pool is right there, the sport field too, every opportunity. Where is that opportunity in Turkey's conditions? There is none. If there is, we will educate him in that comfort.

F: I mean, I am opposed to the system too. Definitely I am worn out, getting nervous. I wish, I say from the beginning I wasn't excited, I wasn't started. But this is not happening with "I wish." Instead of saying too bad (vah vah!) later, I have to pay this two-year bill, I mean. I hope that the end is fine.

F: Not much left. Three months left.

Y: I mean, I . . . because after three months, I will be like a fish out of the water. I will pay another bill that time, because I think that too needs an orientation process. A very pitiful situation.

F: During the first months, I was in a terrible condition. Because it went badly initially, I mean, everything mixed up, fourth grade social, science, I said okay, we went, wondering if we should leave, what we should do, "I won't be able to put this together." Even at night in the bed I prepare a schedule by myself: "How can I get him ready, how can I put him together," you can't take it out of your mind. What if he can't win? Now I live that. I passed that step. Every night I pray to Allah, "How are we going to deal with this if he cannot make it, how will the kid handle it, how am I going to handle it?"

Alternatively, what can we do, where can we go, in which school should we place him? All these are like a net. You struggle with this for two years. At some point it doesn't matter how conscientious the kid, he is still a kid. He says he wants Robert [Lisesi], then when he starts studying, he is "huffing and puffing." You say, "Come on my son, come on my dear"; at some point he loses his energy. You fool the kid: "Come on, you will reach somewhere, you will enter a *kolej* [private school]." If he cannot win, it's a disaster for him, too, because you deceived him for two years. I have the worry of "How can I compensate all this?" I have the fear inside me: "How am I going to deal with it? How am I going to bring him to life? What if he withers? What if he becomes whatever?" You cannot rid your mind of these things.

The range of emotions felt and performed daily, from defiance to resignation, sadness to anger, made daily life difficult for all family members. Exploring this structure of feeling leads along a path of conundrums, paradoxes, and contradictions that interfered with the ability of many families to focus on the practices and strategies that would improve chances to win the test. Working through these sentiments of the family helps to make sense of broader contexts of the actual rules of competition the state imposed on families. The logic of the *sistem*, as the SMSEs are called, is interrogated in chapter 5. The agency of the system and the practices of its agents are scrutinized in chapter 6.

Social Capital in the Service of Human Capital

One way in which to view social capital is through the joint efforts of family members who engage in an accumulation of favors through building social networks. The purpose of this approach is to reproduce the family through a process of accumulation that provides general benefits to an entity that maintains its solidarity. Social capital possessed as a common accumulation accessible (to varying degrees) to all calls attention to the relevance of social forms of solidarity in understanding all forms of organization, including education and the economy. In contrast, the concept of social capital has also been applied to what Bourdieu would refer to as the *individual habitus*, or the complex dispositions of individuals acting in patterned ways in response to various environments, fixed or changing. From this perspective, the embodied individual is a source of interaction with other embodied individuals, capable of change and adaptation. "Like other forms of capital, social capital is productive, making possible the achievement of certain ends [of individuals] that in its absence would not be possible" (Coleman 1988: 91). There is one effect of social capital that is especially important: its effect on human capital in the next generation (Coleman 1988: 98).

Notes

1. See, for example, the entry "aile, (n.) family; household," in Moran 1971: 35. For purposes of census taking, the state uses the official category of "household" (*hanehalkı*) to collect data on the population. Due to the high frequency of households composed of nuclear families that appear in the official Turkish census, the state's official category of *household* has become

mixed with a vernacular use of the word *aile*, further conflating the meaning of *family* with *household*. In common parlance, this conflation occurs in appropriate contexts and results in minimum ambiguity. An exception that sometimes occurs is patrilateral parallel cousin marriage, or the marriage of opposite-sex first cousins related through their fathers who are brothers.

2. By governmentality, "Foucault means the art of government, and signals the historical emergence of distinctive types of rule." (Foucault 1978) He says that government does not "refer to political structures or the management of states" but also designates "the way in which the conduct of individuals or of groups might be 'directed.'" It includes "modes of action, more or less considered and calculated, that [are] destined to act upon the possibilities of action of other people. To govern, in this sense, is to structure the possible field of action of others" (Foucault 1994: 341). Cf. Davies and Bansel 2007: 248.

5

COMPETITION AND CULTURAL REPRODUCTION

We are entering the age of the infinite examination and of
compulsory objectification.
—Michel Foucault, *Discipline and Punish*,
quoted in Allan Hanson, *Testing Testing*.

State, Class, and Education

Istanbul middle-class parents have, for several generations, continued to believe
that elite private middle schools constituted the main path to the best universities and, in turn, increased their children's life chances. Elite middle-school
education was emblematic of a wide range of beliefs about a comfortable material and social life, and a prestigious higher education degree that added value
to the accumulation of a family's symbolic and economic capital. To this day,
elite middle schools, most of them concentrated in Istanbul, represent the symbolic capital of enlightened reason in a secular state. The schools stand as icons
of European sophistication and worldliness in a country that has been increasingly influenced by Euro-American political economy and culture since the
end of World War II. The long history of elite middle schools, their "private-
ness" and their "foreignness," has a social patina of heritage and promise. Over
three generations, the graduates of these schools have added to the accumulation of family reputation and privilege. Alumni of these schools formed tight
cross-generational social networks of mutual support and exchange of favors,
both in Istanbul society and abroad, which continue to provide the social capital
that intersects with economic and cultural-symbolic capital to form a competitive field of education. The field is structurally triangulated by the hegemonic
power of the state to coerce new middle-class families into competition with
each other through the state-instituted private Selective Middle Schools Examination (SMSEs). The state created the structure by setting rules and regulations
for competition among families, but it left to families how they would compete.
Enter the market for test services.

In interviews we conducted in 1996, parents of fifth-graders, comparing their childhood experience with that of their children's, reminisced about the relative absence of competition and the casualness of exam preparation in their generation compared to what they perceived to be an unfair burden placed on them as parents by the state's imposition of the SMSEs when they were introduced in 1983. During the liberalization episode, the Ministry of Education's (MEB) relaxation of its longstanding policy to limit the number of private schools on all levels of the education hierarchy, combined with the privatization of media, greatly increased public exposure to these schools. Their relative scarcity along with rapidly increasing demand for them was a boon to the whole education industry. For those families who could afford them, the test came to be viewed by parents, teachers, school administrators, and education entrepreneurs as both fact and necessity.

For families who enter their children in the private SMSEs, winning the test is a serious matter that absorbs the total energy and resources of the family. The tests became integral, not peripheral, to the accumulation histories of families that participate in this field of competitive class relations. Success or failure in the SMSEs can carry the force of social class inclusion or exclusion from broader fields of competition in Turkish society.

This chapter and the one to follow explore in what ways and to what degree families are their own agents of class reproduction by means of education as these are viewed through the prism of the SMSEs. It focuses on the hegemonic power of the state to impose and enforce rules and regulations on middle-class competition for access to elite schools. It also addresses the ideology of the state as an instrument of power that attempts to control how families, and the public at large, should think about access, fairness, and equity. The chapter is intercalated with the voices of agents of the SMSEs who together provide a framework of discourses on their social construction of reality.

The SMSEs as a Field of New Middle-class Competition

Celia Lury, drawing on the seminal work of the French sociologist Pierre Bourdieu, defines a "field" as a conceptual space in which a game takes place, "a field of objective relations between individuals and institutions who are competing for the same stake" (1996: 88). The SMSEs constitute such a field of competitive play among twenty thousand middle-class families per annum, instituted by the Ministry of National Education through its middle-school test unit. Families are competing for the same stake, namely, winning a place for their child in one of the selective middle schools.

The institutions that objectify the social field are constitutive of the field of objective relations: the state, schools, families, and the market. From the standpoint of a competitive field of social relations, players with more material capital increase their stake in the game over those players with less material capital. The objective collective social class result is an increasing differentiation between new middle-class and core middle-class fragments and their abilities to compete for places in elite schools. From the point of view of Turkey's whole education system, the tests serve as objective instruments for a policy of social exclusion. Istanbul is not only the center of Turkey's growing neoliberal economy—it is also the center of competition among new middle-class families competing to gain access to elite foreign-language middle schools.

Object of the Game

The object of the game is for families to win a place for their child in one of the most prestigious, elite middle schools in the country. Schools are players to the extent that they compete for parents' attention in an effort to attract students with the highest possible test scores that confirm their rank in a relatively stable hierarchy of elite schools. The state establishes the rules of these national tests, imposes its own objective logic on pedagogy and the curriculum, and sets standards for evaluating the test. The governance of rules, pedagogy, and standards of evaluation reside in a centralized unit of the Ministry of National Education in Ankara, the nation's capital. Governance, in the sense of this term used in the previous chapter, refers to the outer boundaries of parents' preferences, but it leaves open the competitive space in which each family considers its preferences framed by its plan of education. The tests are voluntary, evoking the spirit of open access to elite schools, but the system is transparently exclusionary.

Preference and Selection: How It Works

Schools that annually select their cadre of students only by the scores they received on the test became, mutatis mutandis, official "selective" schools. There were two separate but similar tests, one for public Anadolu schools and the other for private schools, both foreign and Turkish. All Anadolu schools were required by the Ministry of National Education to allocate all their places through the Anadolu school test, but private schools had a choice. All the private foreign schools chose to allocate all their places through the private SMSE, but only some private Turkish schools chose to do so. The latter were able to fill their cadres with students of their choice, mainly children whose parents could afford the price. The number of new private Turkish schools that opened during the 1990s created an alternative path to university education, one that allowed well-to-do families a way to avoid both the grueling preparation process of the SMSEs and the fate of ending up in overcrowded and poor-quality public middle schools.

The SMSEs offered universal access to selective schools. Any child in fifth grade who reached age eleven or twelve during the period between two examinations is eligible to enter that year's SMSEs. Parents submit separate application forms for each test, public and/or private, to the examination unit of the Ministry of National Education.

The test format and questions are similar, but differ in minor ways. Both tests consist of one hundred questions to be completed in seventy minutes. The format for both is multiple-choice questions and answers. Both tests are divided into four parts that reflect the third- to fifth-grade curricula of math, Turkish language, science, and social studies (with the alternative of a question on religion). On each test, a student receives a single score to the third decimal place. They differ only in the formula for weighting and scoring the test. A given student's score for the two tests does vary, but students who do well on one test also tend to do well on the other. The all-important examination preparation process is similar for both tests, but preparation strategies vary according to education plans and tactics.

How do students' SMSE scores translate into a hierarchy of selective schools? What begins to make sense of all this is the Ministry of National Education's official Preference and Selection System, whereby a school's selection of a cadre of students and parents' preference for a school come together solely on the basis of the child's score in the examination. For the private schools' test, the state requires that each school set "base points" to establish the minimum number of points a student must score in order to earn a place in that school's contingent. Schools that set higher "base points" are ipso facto more selective. Both individual student scores and schools' base points are published in newspapers across the nation so that parents can strategize how to place a child in the "best" school for a given score. Setting base points is self-correcting over time when the final scores of individual students in a cadre do not meet expectations.

The Preference and Selection System for Anadolu schools as opposed to private schools has some differences. Unlike private schools, which must set minimum base points, Anadolu schools must set a range between maximum and minimum "total weighted standard points." The variance in a school's ceiling and floor can be several hundred points. The result is that Anadolu schools form into an overlapping hierarchy. Their rank order is therefore more ambiguous than that of private schools. As it turns out, the preference system for Anadolu schools is much more restricted and the ranking is less significant in making a choice of schools than that of private schools. Parents or guardians must state their preferences before they know the child's score on the test. In contrast, the preference system for private schools kicks in after the test and publication of scores. Those families that enter their child in both examinations must devise a strategy that takes into account both systems in order to place their child in the "best" school relative to their child's score on both examinations. Families spend endless hours over a long period discussing school preferences in the context of "quality of education" issues.

In 1995, the public SMSE was held on 26 May. That year there were 390 Anadolu schools in the country with a total of 37,724 places. Three hundred thousand children sat for the public SMSE that year. The objective probability of winning a place in an Anadolu school was about one in eight. Other factors affected this probability. The average scores of students in rural areas tend to be lower than the average scores of students in urban areas. Many of the most selective schools in the country are in Istanbul where the concentration of test-takers live.[1]

In metropolitan regions, especially Istanbul, competition is strong, and in Istanbul it is fierce. In the IMV-SAM survey of Turkey's top schools, there were probably fifty top Anadolu schools in all of Turkey, with less than six thousand total places. Of these, twenty-one were in Istanbul, with 2,412 total places. While we do not have the total number of Istanbul students who entered the public SMSE, we conservatively estimate it to be around thirty thousand exam-takers. The objective probability of winning a place in one of the top Istanbul Anadolu schools was only one in twelve. It may have been as low as one in twenty (*Yeni Yüzyıl* 1997: May 22–24).[2]

In 1995, the private SMSE was held five days before the public SMSE. That year there were ninety-four selective private schools in the country with a total of 9,786 places. That year, 17,500 children sat for the private SMSE. The objective probability of winning a place was better than one in two. However, the numbers are deceptive. Sixty-two of the private schools were selective in name only, using the examination as a marketing tool for establishing their "selective" status when a large majority of their students were actually admitted on the basis of their parents' ability to pay. Most of these schools were the result of the government's privatization policy of the 1990s and were owned by Turkish education entrepreneurs. Only a small number of students from these schools were entered in the private SMSE.

From the perspective of families seeking a selective private school that offered foreign-language instruction (a distinguishing characteristic of selective schools), there were only thirty-two schools with a total of 3,691 places that met the quality standard of competitive middle-class families. The objective probability of winning a place in these schools was one in five. At the top of the whole education hierarchy, public and private, were the thirteen private foreign schools with only 1,361 places. The probability of winning a place was less than one in twelve. Ten of the selective private foreign schools with 1,025 places and twelve of the selective private Turkish schools with 1,303 places were in Istanbul. We do not have the actual number of Istanbul exam-takers as a proportion of the total, but it is widely assumed in Turkey that the most intensively competitive site for places in selective private schools in Turkey is Istanbul.

To return to the mechanics of the 1995 national SMSEs from the perspective of the field of competitive social relations, families anxiously awaited the results of the tests. On 16 June, the Ministry of National Education published lists of private SMSE test-takers' scores adjacent to their identification numbers in all the major newspapers of the country. Because the examination preparation process involves endless practice tests that simulate the examination, parents have the information they need to estimate the scores of their children. There is anxiety about the outcome of a performance based on that one day, but they know what to expect. The newspapers give them the first idea of how their child scored relative to all others in the country. There is a period of anxiety as parents wait for the minimum base points established by each private school as its sole criterion of admission policy.

The day after the scores appeared in newspapers, an article appeared that instructed parents about what to pay attention to when making up their list of school preferences. They should first find their child's identification number and write down the total points scored. Then they should look at the "base points" of the schools closest to their child's score to learn how many could be listed. A list of schools, along with their base points and the size of their "contingents" (number of places) was published in the newspapers two days after the publication of students' examination scores. The state Preference and Selection Unit allows a list to have only those schools with base points lower than the student's score. The official form to be filed allows up to seven schools to be listed. These need not be rank ordered, but standard procedure is for parents to put their highest preference first followed by their second preference and so on down the list.

Again we advert to system logic in order to see how the education hierarchy is maintained. How do private schools set their base points? One answer is that they set them by history and tradition. Schools know from previous years' base points and their success rate in attracting a contingent what level of students to expect. Parents' preferences play a part in setting base points, just as expected base points play a part in parents' preferences given their knowledge of how well their child was expected to perform in the SMSEs. The record of past base points set by schools, as well as past scores on examinations, is published by the Ministry of National Education and made available for parents and family members to scrutinize. Except for new schools, the education hierarchy of specific schools (at least those that are most preferred) has been a stable feature of the system that provides near-perfect information for parents. But not all parents acquire the information, and not all parents conform to system rationality in making their preferences. Individual schools also have the information they need to position themselves in the hierarchy, but not all schools have the same strategies. Sometimes they overreach or underestimate. The result is that they may not be able to fill their contingent or can fill it with better scores than they anticipated. The system allows for adjustments of both parents' preferences and schools' base points as the schools' selection of their student contingents proceeds.

To take an example, in 1995, Robert Lisesi set its base points for boys at 652.309. All parents whose children scored above this number could register for a place. Since Robert Lisesi is certain that it will be at or near the top of the preference lists of the highest scoring students, and because it has the list of student scores, it rank orders the list of boys' scores and chooses the top sixty-six boys to fill its contingent. The top of every hierarchy has a clear and near-certain view. If all goes well, the sixty-sixth student selected will have scored 652.309 points, right down to the third decimal place. All others on the Robert list will have scored higher, and the highest score will be the number one score in the nation. In actuality, preferences do vary somewhat, and Robert Lisesi does have competition. Robert instructs in English, the overwhelming language of parental choice and the language in which most schools instruct. Two schools that instruct in German, the private Alman Lisesi and an Anadolu school named Istanbul Lisesi, are Robert's biggest competitors for top-scoring students. Some parents prefer the former because it also teaches English, and others prefer the latter because it is a public school and therefore affordable. In the stable system that has become the private SMSE, each successive school can estimate its relative position in the hierarchy from the size of the contingents and scores of the schools above it. There is a high degree of shared understanding of rankings among parents whom we interviewed.

So far, we have described only the first phase of the Preference and Selection System. Parents have indicated their initial preferences and schools have merely established their place in a market for a pool of candidates that are allocated at that moment. Parents of those test-takers whose points are higher than the base points of the top school on their list can register in that school. This provides new information on the current state of play and begins the next phase. The state allows schools to raise or lower base points. Schools that attract students with scores higher than their base points can raise them. Schools that are having difficulty attracting students lower their base points. Parents are busy watching the movement of base points, often enlisting family members to keep track of the lists of preferred schools so that they can seize the moment before a change. As parents make their choice and commit to one preference, they are withdrawing from all other preferences, opening a place for someone else to occupy.

From the perspective of the MEB, the system works to the extent that parents equate education quality with the base point system only. Put differently, from a system point of view, parents will match their child's test score to the school with the highest possible minimal points and choose that school. This opens places below it for those students with the next highest scores and so on. This approach to placing a child in a school is a form of technical rationality. Were parents' thoughts about whether a school is "right" for their child, or whether the school has this or that reputation, whether it offers a range of amenities and services, whether it fits the personality and interest of the child, or any other criteria, the state's predictability and stability of the preference and selection system would be threatened. More to the point, interviews with parents revealed that they were concerned about making a fit between the subjective evaluation of their child's temperament and their own interest in the qualities of schools.

Notwithstanding parents' subjective evaluation of their child and its fit with a certain kind of school and its pedagogy, most chose a school based on the objective outcome of its ranking. Through informal interviews, we learned that a parent who would not choose the school with the highest score commensurate with the child's score was thought of as "foolish." There can be no stronger evidence of the power of the state to get inside the sanctum of the family and transpose its habitus than this outcome. Technique triumphs over education, a discourse of numbers substitutes for a discourse of reason. The objectification of the family is complete. The cultural logic of the family that treats its members as social persons dissolves into the person as test machine. The discourse of "quality" education is transposed into the discourse of which school is "best" in a rank order of numbers. The work of the classroom is reduced to the work of the lesson school. Knowledge gives way to speed and accuracy.

There is a difference between the selection and preference systems of the two SMSEs. For the public SMSE, parents must file a list of preferred schools before their child takes the test. For the private SMSE, parents file a list of preferred schools after their child has taken the test and the scores of other students are known. Entering both tests creates some complexity and risk for parents who have to consider two different preference and selection systems, but it does little to affect the overall system. Also, parents who could afford private schools may have the option of a good Anadolu school, but parents without money have to rely on winning the Anadolu school test.

The state sets a deadline of two weeks after the publication of the private schools' base points for families to submit their preference list. In 1995, the deadline was 2 July, six weeks after the date of the private SMSE. Each school sets to work making a selection list, poring over the scores of the pool they have attracted and calculating how well they might do. The state requires that each school post its selection results on the same day, which was 11 July. Now begins the bazaar that creates a summer of discontent for many parents. Schools want a full contingent. Parents, with rare exceptions, want to place their child in the most selective school among available alternatives commensurate with the child's score. Over the next eight weeks before the start of the new school year in September, schools raise and lower their base points while parents jockey for position. A place opens up, hurried telephone calls among family members ensue, and someone "wins" the race to register. The whole process, engineered by family members and close friends, requires patience, vigilance, stamina, and coordination. In Istanbul, the schools are spread over the space of the whole city. Parents must be prepared to race to a site and register the child before their closest competitors beat them. In an effort to prevent parents from committing and then bolting to another school, some schools require a nonrefundable cash deposit. Parents who can afford it may hold places in different schools at the same time in an effort to reduce the risk of giving up one place only to find that the other has been taken. Such stories of being left out in the cold, caught between traffic lights, so to speak, are part of the folklore of the private preference and selection system.

In the 1995 private SMSE, parents seemed slow to fill the spaces in some of the private schools, which became worried and began to lower their points almost daily. The difference between initial and final base points is perceived as an indication of where schools stand in the selective private education hierarchy. The bottom of the hierarchy is occupied by schools who use their participation in the system as a market strategy to attract parents who will pay for a place but who also would like to say that their child is in a "selective" school.

Timing is crucial for parents to succeed in their quest for the most selective school available to them. From 12 July to 14 July, a day after schools posted their selection lists in 1995, parents on the original list of a school were allowed to register their child. From this time until the opening of school, each school keeps two lists, one that has a list of students who have registered and the other a list of those who have not. Every time parents register a child, a place becomes available in another school for someone else. Lists change constantly and new lists are posted immediately. This process continues until a final registration deadline. In 1995, that date was 27 August, when all schools were required to send the names of their cadre to the Preference and Selection unit of the Ministry of National Education. There is, however, one consideration that may interfere with the order of this process. The date for parents to register a child who won a place in a preferred Anadolu school was the week of 31 July to 7 August.

The Public Schools Preference and Selection System differs from the private schools system in important ways. The two are as different from each other as the logic of markets is different from the logic of bureaucracies. In April of 1995, before children sat for the public SMSE, parents filled out forms indicating their preferences for particular Anadolu schools and sent them to the Ministry of National Education Selection and Preference System Office in Ankara. The form that year required parents to rank order up to five school choices. For parents, this first step in the examination process is the most important step.

In our interviews, parents emphasized that they must be certain about the first preference they write on the form. The system imposes the following two rules on parents' choice of a school after they learn her or his examination score: a child can be on one and only one school list and only a single change in their preference order is allowed. If parents later change their mind about their first preference, which they are allowed to do after they learn their child's examination score, they cannot return to the former preference. They lose it and the place goes to another child. If they fail to win a place in the school they have substituted for their first choice, the child is blocked from entering any Anadolu school. For example, one parent we interviewed described a case in which a parent wrote down Beşiktaş Anadolu School as his first preference. This is a respected Anadolu school in much demand. Later on, as the process of selection unfolded, it appeared that there would be a chance for his child to win a place in Galatasaray Lisesi, one of the most reputable schools in the hierarchy and a choice near the top of most parents' lists. But at that point other rules came into play. Here, a brief digression will help the reader explore the logic of the system.

The system, totalizing as it appears, does not follow its own internal consistent technocratic logic. Metropolitan geopolitics also comes into play. For example, exam-takers in Istanbul *must* choose three schools in Istanbul and are allowed to write down on the form two schools in Ankara *or* Izmir, but not both. The reason is that Istanbul students have higher average scores than the national average. Also, the number of Istanbul students who sit for the examination is much larger than the numbers in these other cities. Given the intense competition in Istanbul and the lower probability of winning a top school, some Istanbul parents look to schools in Ankara and Izmir, where the competition is less intensive and where there is a higher probability of obtaining a place in a top school.

Part of the folklore of the system consists of stories of Istanbul parents who send their child to live with a relative in another city for the sole purpose of taking the examination and winning a place in a better school than the child is expected to win in Istanbul. A loophole in the system allows a student to later transfer back to a more desirable school in Istanbul. Exam-takers who live anywhere other than in Istanbul are free to take places in any school in the country, including in Istanbul. This equity issue is one of the few deviations from system logic and mechanics of the SMSEs.

The 1995 public SMSE was held on 26 May, five days after the private SMSE. After the scores are tabulated in Ankara, schools receive from the state the names and scores of those students whose parents listed them as their first preference, second preference, and so on to the fifth preference. Each school looks at the names on its list, their scores, and then computes maximum and minimum "Total Weighted Standard Points" (*Toplam Ağırlıklı Standard Puan* [*TASP*]). The result is a range between two numbers. After the state has allocated to each school the number of places that will comprise its contingent, each school makes an original registration list.

Before schools post their original registration lists, the state publishes two kinds of information in newspapers around the country. The first kind of information is about the size of each school's contingent for all the Anadolu schools in Turkey. Parents can find the schools that are on their preference list and know the size of every school's contingent by the number of student identification numbers listed under each school. The second kind of information is another list of all the schools that gives for each school the range between its maximum and minimum TASP.

In this first phase of preference and selection, some parents now have the basic information they need to choose a school. Parents whose children's examination score falls between the maximum and minimum TASP of schools that are on their original preference form filed in April may register their child. They have a guaranteed place and the process of preference and selection has come to an end. In 1995, original list registration of students occurred the week of 31 July to 7 August. As mentioned above, in the Private Preference and Selection process, many parents are maneuvering to improve their child's prospects to earn a place in a more selective school. If the child also took the public SMSE, parents need to weigh, in a short space of time, the value they place on a particular selective Anadolu school relative to a particular selective private school.

Each Anadolu school also composes a waiting list. Recall that parents were allowed one change on their preference form. Like practically every other step in the process of preference and selection, the state had a rule. To make a change, parents had to have their registration form stamped with an official seal that indicates they relinquished their hold on their first preference and substituted it with another. In stark contrast to the neoliberal atmosphere of the private Preference and Selection System, where parents could hold onto several options while maneuvering for gain, the public Preference and Selection System precluded such maneuvering.

The private system was more open to competition, but in this instance less risky than the public system. Parents who have made a change in their preference form begin a part of the process referred to as the "open contingent" phase, which goes on until the final registration period on the opening day of school in early September. The open contingent process begins when schools post their first open contingent notice inviting applications from parents with eligible children (based on their exam score in relation to schools' maximum and minimum TASP) to preregister. Several days later, schools make a cut in those applications and invite some parents to register their child. In 1995, the first open contingent notices were posted on school grounds at 5:30 PM on 7 August, followed by a period of application from 7–19 August. A second round of open contingent notices, followed by invitations to apply, occurred from 23–25 August. There were three more rounds before a final registration on opening day of school.

Return briefly to the parent who had preferred the prestigious Galatasaray Lisesi to Beşiktaş Anadolu School, making this change on his preference form, the only one allowed by the system. He had given up a secure place in Beşiktaş Anadolu in which his daughter appeared on the "original registration list," to gamble for a more selective school by placing his daughter on Galatasaray's "open contingent list." According to the parent who told us this story, "the girl's parents had assessed all the available information beforehand and decided to go for it." Everything looked favorable. There were open places, and the child's examination score had positioned her near the top of the first open contingent list of one of the oldest and most venerable education institutions in Istanbul and all of Turkey. But as luck would have it, in the last half hour of the registration period that would fill the contingent, a flood of parents whose child had scored higher made a quick switch themselves to Galatasaray open contingent list, moving ahead of the girl.

The parent who told us the story explained that the story was "instructive" because "the system now locked the child out of an Anadolu school." She could neither register at Galatasaray nor return to register at Beşiktaş. This story of a real case no doubt will enter the folklore of SMSEs and fulfill its allegorical function of warning against reaching too high. But "What was the allegory?" we inquired, naively presuming it to be about overreaching. Embarrassed for us, the father quietly drew his conclusion that "Parents must use all the information available to them to put their first preference first and to have a realistic picture of the system." By "realistic," it turned out, he meant "having all the quantitative data on the history of final average points for each school and a probability statement of the child's examination score based on simulations of past performance on practice tests as an index of performance on the real exam."

One can imagine the intricacies of strategy and tactics associated with the preference and selection process, and how much stress and anxiety it places on children, parents, and other family members. Within the broader scheme of things, at least these families had the privilege of struggle. The vast majority of several million families of fifth-graders in Turkey had self-selected out of the system long before there ever was a question about inclusion among the three hundred thousand families that aspired to join the ten to fifteen thousand real winners. The large majority of parents who entered their child in this race were official "losers" from the start. The preparatory examination scores of their children were too low even to contemplate inclusion in the final outcome. These children would end up back where they began, in state public middle schools or nonselective private middle schools, where the odds of attaining university education in Turkey would be against them.

Metadiscourse, Counterdiscourse, and Media Discourse

The power of the state to control access to selective schools through its imposition of the SMSEs, thereby regulating every school's selection of students and parents' preferences for schools, relies for its legitimacy on the symbolic power of its ideology. What holds true for one subsystem holds true for the others. Each form of agency has its own critique of the system but also its own reasons for playing the game. The SMSEs are perceived by the players to be both necessary and despicable.

Metadiscourse

The metadiscourse of the SMSE has two keywords—*sistem* and *objektif.* The Turkish words are borrowed from English—system and objective. The monologic of an objective system is that it is absolute and totalizing within its claims, as opposed to a dialogic that requires a dialogue of two or more participants to resolve any claims. The SMSE system and its subsystems constitute a discourse of state domination that has the presumption of claims to mechanical efficiency, internal coherence, and precision. These are established by quantifiable measures and methods that are taken at their face value as being objective, or thinglike, a reality external to the mind and therefore outside the realm of being something that can be challenged or interrogated. Applied to the SMSE system, the design of the tests calls for multiple choice questions and answers. Answers are objectified as limited in scope and having only one right answer. Performance on the test is evaluated objectively by assigning a number to the third decimal place. These scores are the only criterion used for ranking all students on a linear scale. Students' scores are used to create a hierarchy of schools on a similar scale. This reasoning is carried throughout all parts of the system.

The system has its own objective "truth." The MEB claims that the system is "fair" because it is objective. All schools and families are treated within the same rules and regulations in the same way at every step of the process, from enrollment in the tests to the allocation of the last place in the selective schools. The state requires that every enrolled child in the country take the test on the same day and at the same time. The test can be taken only once, which avoids any accusation of unfair treatment. The state provides the maximum amount of information on rules, regulations, and procedures as well as making public all its quantitative results. Complete information that is universally available to all supports the MEB claim of fairness and equity. The SMSEs are the perfect example of what is meant by a modern society. Power is faceless and blind in its mission of equal opportunity within the framework of its own objective logic.

Counterdiscourse of the system is best left to narratives of the nonstate agents who are the players in the field of competitive social relations—public commentators, school administrators, teachers, tutors, and owners of lesson schools. Educators, school entrepreneurs, administrators, and teachers who produce education services for the SMSEs are more informed and articulate about the intricacies of the system than are parents, who see themselves as consumers of institutionalized education and test services. Multiple perspectives on education and test services, and critiques of the system, arise from agents' special interests and their respective locations in the field of competitive social relations. Whether agents accommodate or resist the system, they must come to terms with the power of the state to regulate and control their activities. Opting out or ignoring the rules is not an option.

The remainder of this chapter explores how agents in the SMSE field of competitive social relations perceive themselves in relation to the objective system and to each other. It draws on narrative accounts of different agents from the standpoint of their competing and, at times, conflicting interests. Major fault lines of competition and conflict are the following: public and private schools, public and private teachers, "education" schools and "lesson" schools, all of the above and tutors.

The SMSEs brought a small and relatively unobtrusive area of Istanbul social life into the consciousness of the nation through the magic of media and promotion. The chapter concludes with comments on portrayal of the SMSEs as hyperreality and a form of commodity fetishism.

Counterdiscourse

Abbas Güçlü received his degree from Ankara University's highly regarded Gazi School of Education. He began his career working for the editor of an education movement magazine in the early 1980s, and became the first journalist in Turkey to have a regular newspaper column on education when he joined Istanbul's *Milliyet Gazetesi* around 1985. He continues to write the regular education page for that newspaper and is one among only a few journalists in the country writing a regular column on education issues. In an excerpt from our interview, he comments on the root dilemma of the majority of families that enter "the race":

> The exam system is not beneficial to society. But in a system like this where 300,000 students enter [the public SMSE] and 30,000 students get in . . . This is even worse in the university [entrance examination] where there are 2.5 million entries. The number of students accepted to good universities is about 200,000. That is, you have to eliminate. . . . We can't accept [students into middle school and university] by looking at their success in elementary school or in middle school like they do in Germany. Here, let alone the difference in education between areas, even the difference in education in two different parts of Istanbul is very different. If you say you are going to accept students according to their success in [previous] schools there will be big problems. The exam system is not good or nice, but at least it is reliable. In this exam, they say that everybody, no matter if you are from the elite class or if you are rich, will take this exam and if he/she succeeds, he/she will get in [a selective middle school]. I think it is beneficial that [the exam] continues because it creates equality and reliability.

Güçlü defends the fairness of an objective system because it is "necessary" and "reliable." He also believes that the system is not "beneficial to society" but

thinks it is beneficial because it creates "equality." *Equality* in this context refers
to a guarantee to parents that a given score on the test will result in a given
place in the system of selection. These apparently contradictory statements reflect the construction of economic, social, and cultural reality, not muddled
thought or confusion.

Birkan Yetkin, former teacher, founder, and education administrator of private
schools, is an education entrepreneur. She also is a leader in delivering a progressive education alternative to the children of new middle-class families. In an
excerpt from our interview, she rejects the very principles upon which the SMSEs
are founded:

> The SMSE is my wound. There even was one year when we resisted entering the
> SMSEs, but the quality of the schools that take students through SMSEs test scores
> are more respected [than schools that don't participate]. Even though I resisted
> strongly, we went back to the exam system. As an educator, I am opposed to this
> [test]. The system is so corrupt. The student who enters our school with the high-
> est points [in the SMSEs] can't do [our] compositions because he only thinks me-
> chanically. I oppose this [test], but the government couldn't solve it. The result of
> the SMSEs is that the child is emotionally worn out from a never-ending exam. I
> mean at the first grade of elementary school, a test book is prepared.

The oppositional discourse of education versus the test appears in nearly all debate and commentary, but varies in meaning according to context. Birkan is in
the private sector, competing with lesson schools [*dershane*] and tutors as alternatives that parents weigh when they are shaping their strategy for winning the
test. Her comments are aimed directly at the impact of the SMSEs on the ability
of private primary schools to satisfy parents' demand that their children receive
quality education *and* preparation for the test. In her view, as an educator, the
two are in conflict. She tried to remain outside the test system but was forced
back into it. The state, through the SMSEs, equates quality education with selective education, in effect privileging test results over pedagogy. Parents prefer
pedagogy over testing, which presents a dilemma for them that is explored in
the next chapter.

Lale Ünal has a graduate degree in education from Boğaziçi University in
Istanbul. She is a self-identified leader of the progressive education and private
schools movement and recent founder and education administrator of a private
primary and middle school. It is not surprising that she shares Birkan's concerns and adds some of her own:

> The SMSE is shameful and nasty, a pretext because to do well or to make a mistake
> is merely of the moment, without knowing or not knowing, but without giving the
> child her or his rights. My anger begins at this point. These rights are only a set of
> private lesson situations. We do what will give them the least harm, knowing that
> we are in a system.

When Lale refers to "private lesson situations," she means the distraction
of teaching to the test as if it were education. What is shameful to Lale is the

pretension of the test and all the anguish and effort that she and her clients (parents) have to endure. Personally, she feels compromised. The test is "inside" her school because of parental demand, when her pedagogy is completely at odds with it. There is "fact" and "necessity"—the fact of the test and the necessity of the pretense. Private primary school administrators believe that the test must be embedded in quality education to be meaningful when in reality the test merely focuses on a multiple-choice answer to a multiple-choice question. In this act, learning is reduced to technique. It is "of the moment." Teaching to the test is "shameful and nasty," a pretext because it falls outside of learning and knowledge as education pedagogy would have it. Her competitors are private lesson schools outside the classroom and tutors that teach only to the test.

Vitali Meşulam has a master's degree in chemistry and a job in a chemical company. He also is a well-known and much sought-after private tutor of primary school children whose parents have entered them in the SMSEs. His beautiful home, nestled in an exclusive district of new middle-class housing developments near the Bosphorus, also serves as his classroom and office. Like most tutors, parents find him through their social networks. He tutors a small number of students, testing them for selection. Those he selects from administering a test "are matched as equal in groups of two so that they compete against each other and do their homework."

> Of course the tests are not unjust. It is the system, I mean, I cannot think of a better system. There is none. There won't be. How can it be? You give an exam, there's no other way. But this system is very bad right now . . . because there are too many 100s [perfect scores]. How are we going to distinguish them? Can you tell the difference? They [test makers] turned this [test] into information control rather than a test. There are four books: two science, two social science [science includes math]. That is where all the difference is. They are right, too. Why? Because if they ask for talent [aptitude], many schools don't have labs, etc., parents will say "equal opportunities," and so on. I find this aspect of the system right because there is nothing else to do. One question [answered wrong] really makes a difference of 300 people in a 300,000-people test. I know the standard deviations . . . In a test with one hundred questions . . . a few wrong answers can eliminate most test-takers from the private foreign schools. Let me tell you that there are five hundred very good kids that can all score above 94 [out of 100]. Failure to get into a good private foreign school is viewed as ruinous among ambitious families.

Of interest in this narrative is the discourse of techno-speak—a discourse of numbers, probabilities, and conclusions drawn from statistical analysis of the system. Vitali understands the system logic and reason for being. Its justification is in the formal elegance of a system that can select out the maximum number of students. The only flaw is that there are too many students who can achieve the highest score. The perfect system would be one that had no two students with the highest score. The solution to this flaw is to raise the bar, to increase the difficulty of the test. What is not present in Vitali's narrative is any expression of the concerns expressed by public and private school educators or parents as consumers of quality education.

Ergüder Pasin is a graduate of the Economic and Commercial Sciences Academy. He has spent most of his working life in commercial trade—first with a company that sells construction equipment, working as a sales manager, later going into business with his own stores. He does not call himself a "teacher." Like many tutors, his interest in tutoring "grew as a hobby":

> I tutored on Saturdays and Sundays. The store stayed along with tutoring on Saturdays and Sundays. We saw that was being successful. Then, this happened with the pressure of friends. "Hey, take a look at my child, too!" It continued like that. It is fun. You enjoy it, to protect the child from the pressure in the neighborhood. The children become the victims of this wheel. On one hand, it is good; on the other hand, it is not. The race, I mean, is really among five thousand students, among the children who can have a private education. Now this has been growing every year . . . during my son's graduation the number of students who can win the Anadolu *lisesi* [middle school] went up to 200,000. The number of *kolejler* [private foreign middle schools] didn't change. A lot of Anadolu schools opened. But as long as the number of private foreign schools doesn't change, they *can't* change, the demand for these schools increases. Everybody runs to enter those schools. I don't count the private Turkish schools, they can be entered without the SMSEs, but even some of those participate in the SMSEs. Really, in Turkey today, in order to work at a good place in good conditions, they look only at very good qualifications. I mean, to gain those qualifications, I think a child should spend half his life in school. In Turkey, the number of chosen students, quality students, shows an arithmetic increase. The population increase of the other middle schools is geometric.

Media Discourse

The tests and the people who were involved in them would appear to be unlikely candidates for media exposure were it not for the dispossession of state-owned public media and communications and their privatization as a result of the growing neoliberal economy. In the language of news media and the promotion industry, the SMSEs produced stories that had "legs." In the 1990s, the SMSEs became an annual nationwide event. The popular name for the SMSEs is *yarış*, which means "race." Hundreds of thousands of families were going through the agonizing process of preparing their children for the competition while many of their friends and neighbors who had experienced its trials and tribulations relived the experience as neighbors, friends, and co-workers. Media greatly magnified the "value" and significance of the experience. The SMSEs, often referred to in interviews with parents using the English word "fiasco" (*başarısızlık*), smacked of soap opera. Mothers were at the center of a vortex that would drag them down like a dark cloud or a cloud that could lift them to the sky if only they could win the test for their child.

Simultaneously, emotions that persisted for several years after the test were expressed as lamentation over lost childhood, or before the test, a dogged determination to triumph over other mothers. In the gendered discourse of test preparation, most fathers disappeared from the field of battle, leaving the work, management, and responsibility to their wives while they alternately receded into denial or reappeared to challenge the right of the state to interfere in their own and their family's social life. Families suffered emotionally from being under the pressures of the system for a lengthy period of one to three years of preparation and anxiety. Fathers often commented sarcastically that "the family takes the test" before returning to their metaphorical cocoons. The SMSE, a "dinosaur" in Lale Ünal's words, created a hyper-real atmosphere. At times it seemed as if the whole aura surrounding the test was similar to a high-stakes bet, an exciting gamble against the odds but then also a kind of desperation that became a rite of passage and badge of courage for the whole family.

The objective statistical probability of winning a place in a private foreign school was perceived as low, fueling a "need" to seek maximum market expertise at a premium. Winning, therefore, took on the character of "triumph" against long odds. By 1995, parents were aware that the number of places in Istanbul private schools had increased to over nine thousand, and that some private schools were experiencing open places at the close of the official selection process. They also knew that some private schools chose not to participate in the national test, lowering their stature but providing an alternative way in which to avoid entering their child in a public school. Private schools could be safety valves and provide a protective social environment for their children as well as the family as a whole. The cast of characters grew over time as a number of schools, lesson schools, teachers, and tutors acquired celebrity status for their phenomenal test success. The adulation for a "super tutor" was as extraordinary as the tutor's actual technique was ordinary. The intense pressure the state put on the shoulders of eleven-year-old children was a national scandal, a disgrace that would end in loss of childhood that could never be recovered.

Symbolic Capital, Commodity Fetishism, and Celebrity Status

Neoliberal ideology goes hand in hand with a global ideology of consumer culture promoted through electronic media. The test became a commodity fetish. By fetishizing the test, some would say making it a spectacle, making celebrities of its child winners and wizards of its newly wealthy test services experts, media helped to create and promote a public consumer subculture that enhanced the symbolic capital of the new middle class. The test was a symbolic rite of passage that justified the prestige and privilege accorded to its winners and held out the promise of a comfortable consumer life that was visible in the postmodern culture of the city and portrayed in television programs and other media. Private media were themselves a product of neoliberal policy. Prior to 1980, there were only two or three state television channels. Fifteen years later, the world had come to Istanbul and entered into homes through radios, televisions, magazines, and newspapers. Media moguls appeared and delivered huge audiences to advertisers and their corporate clientele.

Three material phenomena influenced the rise of a promotional symbolic culture surrounding the SMSEs' field of competitive social relations. First was the nationalization of elite middle school selectivity, an appropriation of the private schools' prerogative to choose whomever they wanted. The state entered the field of play on the lofty ground of secular republican égalité. Second came an intensification of competition within the middle class over the demand for quality education and the ability of families to pay a high price for reproducing social class in lira, sweat, social sacrifice, and personal well-being. Third, privatization of the media and subsequent media competition led to a hyper-realization of all aspects of the exam process.

For example, television shows such as *Towards the Exam* on HBB at 5:45 PM received call-ins from its viewers, producing an interactive framework in which parents could evaluate and further consider the information and advice obtained from family, friends, and neighbors. The Ministry of National Education's *Radio Club*, a program airing broad education issues, also devoted time to the mechanics of the tests. But most important to a promotional culture were the national daily newspapers and weekly magazines that competed with each other by sensationalizing the SMSEs in dramatic headlines and hyper-real stories on all aspects of the test system. Meanwhile, the education sections of newspapers expanded their space as columnists offered frequent advice and commentary on every aspect of the process leading up to the test. Education crises in previous decades had been aired, so to speak, in the streets or not at all. But during the liberalization episode, folklore was transformed into its "modern," commoditized forms. It became hyper-realized and overvalued.

Consider, for example, the elevated symbolic status that became attached to SMSE "winners." To attract the attention of their readers, newspapers promote the examinations as a "contest" (*yarışma*) with "winners" (*kazananlar*) whose photos appeared in the paper along with a short story. The newspaper *Milliyet* (31 May 1995) placed on its front page a photo of two boys holding and hugging each other. The caption underneath reads "Super Twins of Examination." This is not the real SMSE, only a facsimile created by the newspaper to attract readers. The full story of the "super twins" appears on an inside page, which begins with the information that the twins attend Istanbul Lütfi Banat Primary School. Human interest in nature versus nurture lies in the fact that they "resemble each other and fit together like a T." One of them answered 96 of 100 questions correctly in the newspaper's fifth sample private schools test and 99 of 100 questions correctly in the sample public schools test. His brother answered 95 and 98, respectively.

The topic of twins presented an opportunity for *Milliyet* to pose one of the most frequently asked questions about examination preparation: "All right, what is the secret of this success?" Many parents who are readers of *Milliyet* no doubt hoped that the secret would be in the genes, absolving them of collective guilt for "not doing enough." *Milliyet* goes straight to the core with questions like "Is it a tutor? A lesson school?" The surprising, but ultimately deflating, answer in this case is "Neither one." The twins are quoted as saying "We are learning lesson to lesson, we pay serious attention, and we study our lessons five hours every day." No doubt readers who are mothers are praying that it takes only hard work. Fathers in denial are hoping that the child can win without breaking the family bank. Unfortunately, when the reader probes farther, it turns out that the twins did study with both tutors and lesson schools, but in the newspaper account they emphasize the importance of their own study habits. Parents need to do anything necessary to provide the child with a small advantage when a single mistake could easily mean failure to enter a preferred school—commonly referred to in interviews as "one question, one school."

The twins report that they both want to enter Istanbul High School, which readers will readily recognize as a *public* school that has one of the highest success rates for placing students in universities through the university entrance examination. *Milliyet* tells readers that their father is a chemical engineer and their mother a pharmacist. Enter social class. What parents will certainly take from this story is the name of the primary school, the school that the winners want to enter, the knowledge about the parents' education, and the grim "fact" of five hours of study every day for months, if not the whole year.

General readers are likely to be attracted to the idea of a "contest" that can produce young "champions," as they are referred to in *Milliyet*. Both general readers and parents will interiorize the notion of "test success" as the most important concept in education. Lesson school trumps elementary school, which unmasks the displacement of what teachers refer to as education (*eğitim*) with pedagogy (*öğretim*). What is unremarkable, because it is so universally accepted and internalized, is that "test success" is a cultural concept most closely associated with social destinations desired by new middle-class families.

By the time the real SMSE is held at the end of the school year in late May, readers will have been prepared for receiving national "champions." *Milliyet* (16 June 1995) published a photo of a boy raising his arms above his head with the caption "Private School Champion from a State School." The perceived improbability of this event, which nevertheless happens, is the attraction for many readers because it holds the promise of individual upward mobility. The formula becomes repetitive, satisfying questions that are general to the whole system. Readers will pay attention to the name of the boy's primary school (Istanbul Turhan Mediha Tansel Ilkokulu), the highest points (669.564), what school he will enter, what his father does for a living (his wife and he were *memur*, lower-level white-collar employees of a bank before they retired), and how he prepared (he was learning lesson to lesson) are being carefully noted. Readers will take special notice of the champion's comments to the effect that he did not neglect entertainment and playing games, nor did he work all of the time. This claim appeals because it is counterintuitive to the "test machines" strategy and contrasts with the common approach of treating preparation for the tests like generals prepare for a war. His father is quoted as saying flatly: "Our material basis isn't sufficient for my son to be taught at a private school. This is why I want him to win an Anadolu school." As it turned out, earlier in the story his son told the reporter that he entered the private schools examination in order to become prepared for the public Anadolu school examination, and added, "But I want very much to study at Robert Lisesi." This result expresses poignantly the dilemma of the majority of core middle-class families in Istanbul who share in the aspirations of the upper middle class but do not rise to the level of its material conditions. Victory for a champion from the core middle class can be bittersweet.

The Ministry of National Education participates in creating a spectacle by holding a ceremony and public event to announce the top winners. This event is covered by national media and is of promotional interest to winning schools and tutors who share the limelight. The top winners were announced not only by their own name, the name of their primary school, and their preferred middle school, but they also appeared often in a photograph with their tutor. When the 1995 Anadolu school test results were published, 5 students out of 295,944 received the highest score with identical points (861.850). This in itself was newsworthy on several counts. Multiple identical top scores signal to next year's parents that the bar for entrance is being raised. Competition is intensifying.

The top score also attracts personal interest. What is a top scorer like, and more importantly, what is his or her social location and habitus? One of the winners was singled out because he is the son of one of Turkey's prominent industrial families. In this case, name recognition was an important part of the story. *Cumhuriyet* (6 July 1995) published a photo in which the boy appeared not only with his well-known parents but also with his tutor. Nevertheless, use of the recognizable family name to promote the event came only in the minor headline that announced that the son of the industrial magnate placed first in the test.

The level of competition in Istanbul is the most intense in the country, where the competitive market for newspapers is also the "hottest." The main headline accompanying the above story of the Istanbul boy who was winner was "Istanbul is Weighty in Anadolu Schools," which referred to the confirmation, once again, of the disproportionate success rate of test-takers living in Istanbul as well as preferences for Istanbul schools from parents residing outside Istanbul. This particular story points out that nine of the top ten winners will enter Istanbul high schools, and that eight of those will enter Istanbul Erkek Lisesi, an old prestigious public school that predates the era of Anadolu schools. Its reputation for offering a demanding education and one that requires both German- and English-language teaching is unparalleled. The story concludes with the "examination statistic" that seven of the ten "most preferred" public schools in the country, according to parent preference forms submitted to the Student Placement Results Center prior to the public SMSE, are in Istanbul. Likewise, eight of the top ten winners in the private SMSE come from Istanbul.

Milliyet's headline of a story on the Istanbul winners with perfect scores on the public SMSE read "100% Super Students." The middle schools that select "Super Students" are given equally hyper-realized designations, such as Robert Lisesi, which one newspaper trumpeted as "Five-star Robert." Schools reap symbolic capital created by media promotion. In 1996, when the average household income of the middle quintile of Istanbul's income distribution was $14,084, Robert's tuition was $13,000! Robert was able to charge 16 percent higher tuition than Koç High School, the second highest tuition at $11,000, and 33 percent higher tuition than public Istanbul Erkek Lisesi. The average household income of the fourth quintile was $21,482. These figures reflect the increasing differentiation between middle and upper middle-class families. New and upper middle-class families who place their children in the best schools are becoming more like the lower tier of the upper class. Even a very "comfortable" Istanbul household in the fourth quintile would pay 60 percent of its annual income in tuition to Robert. The lowest tuition for a private foreign school in 1996 was $4,900.

A Note on the Meaning of "Access" and "Equity"

By 1995, the education crisis of the new and upper middle class—the proximate causes for which could be found in the economic policies of the liberalization episode that had begun in 1980—had become internalized in some Istanbul middle-class families as an examination hell. The examination system, in all its dimensions, had become an objective instrument of struggle, an instrument for drawing increasingly distinct boundaries between fragments within a changing middle class. The SMSEs were divided into two tests, each with its own competitive conditions, internal logic, and practices that deepened the chasm between those who could afford to compete and those who could not. Those families entering the private SMSE were self-selected by ability to pay money, reducing the number of entrants to less than 6 percent of the total number of public SMSE entrants. Over half of the private SMSE entrants would find a place in a selective private school, but only one in ten public SMSE entrants would find a place in an Anadolu school. The two systems therefore differed in their intensity of competition and their objective probabilities of success, to the relative disadvantage of those upper middle-class families that could not afford accelerating costs of the competition. At the same time, most of the upper middle-class entrants to the private SMSE had low-cost access to the public SMSE, in effect achieving another competitive advantage over their public school counterparts that doubly disadvantaged the latter. And to add insult to injury, a triple disadvantage was inflicted on middle-class families that used only public schools when private schools began to raid public schools for teachers who seemed to have the power to make a difference in outcomes. But even a triple competitive disadvantage was not the end of the suffering of these families. There was yet another disadvantage in the differential access to the market for education services in what had become a veritable market for creating test machines.[3]

By all accounts, the creation and execution of the SMSEs resolved the important class issue of access to quality middle-school education. The selection and preference subsystem left little or no room for corruption or special treatment. Performance in the tests mechanically determined a final distribution of scores among competing schools. The selection process handled thousands of transactions as outcomes unfolded in a genuine drama of competition and achievement. At the end of the process, every family test-taker knew where he or she stood. The final act was performed when every school sent its list of admissions to an office of registration in the MEB. Everything about the objective system, from creation and management to availability of information and results, was visible in the public domain.

What the objective system does not resolve, with one important exception, is the issue of equity. The exception has to do with the variable quality of education in the nation's public schools. The course of study in primary schools in Turkey is standardized nationwide. Primary school children have the same teacher through all five grades. Teacher training is also the prerogative of the MEB, reinforcing other forms of standardization. The MEB rejected aptitude or cognitive ability in favor of a test anchored in what students learned, i.e., knowledge and achievement. The four categories of knowledge are in math, language, science, and social science. There are four books used universally in classrooms and constitute a common source for those families who are preparing for the SMSEs. Two are math and science and two are Turkish language and social science. Most parents, and indeed all agents of the private market for test services, interpolated this configuration as two "abstract" subjects and two "factual" subjects. The relevance of this classification for test scores is that subject areas and particular questions are weighted differently. A common perception among parents is that math and language are easier subjects to prepare for because they have absolute values, i.e., definite answers in multiple-choice format. In contrast, answers to social science questions are believed to be more arbitrary, therefore more susceptible to guesses that lead to wrong answers in a multiple choice format.

The issue of equity, however, is not addressed through a process of standardizing what in practice is a variation in quality education among the nation's primary schools. Equity also is not addressed by the objective fairness of the SMSEs. Ironically, the objective system that replaced favoritism within a circle of privileged families by creating a level playing field for middle-class competition opened the door to the development of a neoliberal market for preparation services. The competition shifted to a heated-up, overpriced market for preparation services. For families of fortune whose children were incapable of competing in the SMSEs, the neoliberal economy generated growth in private Turkish schools that provided a comfortable alternative without the pain.

Notes

1. These are 1995 figures culled from information in FKM Lesson School booklets prepared for distribution to parents whose children had enrolled for test lessons.
2. IMV-SAM is a civil administration foundation and social research center interested in promoting and funding private foreign-language education. In May 1997, the foundation placed articles in the newspaper *Yeni Yüzyıl* on the results following the completion of a recent research on Turkey's best middle schools.
3. Ironically, education returned to political crisis in the streets of Istanbul in the spring of 1997, when crowds, mostly Islamists, marched against a government proposal to extend compulsory education from five to eight years. They viewed the decision, long in the making as a part of a standardization of education levels sought by the Organization for Economic Cooperation and

Development, as an attack on religious schools that would be unable to teach the Koran. For a moment, interest turned into realpolitik when the Eight Grade Reform, as it was called, became the issue through which parliamentary politics tested the relative power of secularist versus Islamist political ideologies and strategies.

6

PREPARING TO WIN A PLACE

> What will this economic sector create in the end? The rich class has a private tutor sector. The parent is very determined too, more determined than the child. The child goes from one tutor to another, and at the end the child is mentally tired, fed up, and becomes a test machine.
>
> —Birkan Yetkin, educator, owner and administrator
> of a private progressive school.

> I mean, *kurs* teacher, *etüd* teacher, *özel* teacher—these are all different. There are teachers just for teaching technique. The teacher or tutor says, "My job is the technique."
>
> —Cihan Aksoy, frustrated father
> of an eleven-year-old son.

> A kid's mother, being a very ambitious mother, prepares him very well for two years and she is very successful. Then he enters the exam. In the exam room the kid does not touch the test paper. There are the questions. He has a pencil in his hand. He doesn't do anything. The teacher says, "Son, it started. Start." No sound from the boy. They call his mother. His mom comes quickly. "Son, why aren't you starting?" He replies, "I did everything you wanted until now, I studied. Now I don't want to answer these questions."
>
> —A story told by Jale, mother of a child preparing for
> the Selective Middle School Examinations (SMSEs).

New middle-class parents viewed the SMSEs as an invasion of family privacy and violation of the rights they assert over dominion of the conjugal family, particularly over childhood, but also the freedom to live their social lives without interference from the state. Some parents, mostly fathers, were emotional over loss of intimacy within their conjugal relationship. Loss of childhood, social alienation, and threat to conjugal intimacy were portrayed in narratives as "sacrifices" almost too great to bear. Too great, that is, but for one overarching value: winning places in private foreign-language schools that teach in foreign languages using foreign teachers. Private Turkish schools were included to the extent that they could copy the ideal type.

Families with an accumulation history of multiple capitals—economic, social, and cultural-symbolic—had the most to gain and the best chance of winning places in the most highly valued schools. New middle-class families that embraced neoliberal ideas and an ideology of consumerism on a global scale of capitalist growth and competition were positioned to compete for these schools. These and other class issues come to light during the process of preparing children for the SMSEs, the main focus of this chapter.

The root problem for families who compete to win the SMSEs is developing a winning strategy that includes test preparation. Over time, demand for one type of school increased faster than supply despite new schools, further intensifying competition among a growing number of new middle-class families. To solve this problem, families included in their strategy expert services outside the home, stimulating a private market for expert test services. As family strategies that included market expertise increased test scores, the Ministry of National Education ratcheted up the difficulty of the test questions in order to regulate access to the most desirable schools by keeping numbers of admission at a near constant percentage of test-takers. The result was an even more competitive environment for families, stimulating an even greater demand for better expert services. The cost of upscale market services soared, excluding most middle-class families from serious competition while stretching even the budgets of many new middle-class families. A relatively small number of elite private service providers were able to grow and accumulate private wealth to the point where the state's national accounts included these services as a separate economic sector. This chapter is focused on the agency of the neoliberal market for test services and the struggle of new middle-class families to win the private SMSE by creating strategy options and putting them into practice.

Market Segmentation by Class Fragments and by Market Agents

For purposes of analysis and interpretation, we classify the market for test services in two ways. One is by *class fragment*, the other by *market agents*. The market for test services is segmented within the middle class. Fragments are best delineated by their accumulation of multiple capitals pooled by families, not individuals. A family's education plan begins years in advance of the test; many parents say, "at birth." A child's education is an ever-present topic when families are alone or together with friends and relatives. The subject finds its way into conversation on social occasions intended for other purposes. As families come closer to the year of reckoning, the test becomes an obsession as parents stiffen their resolve to win.

Family aspirations are relative to a particular fragment within the middle class. Those families with accumulation histories that consist of multiple capitals are most likely to rise to the top. In core and lower middle-class families, parents have only limited material and cultural capital. Their quest for quality education is likely to focus on their preference for any Anadolu school that would allow them to avoid entering their child in an overcrowded public classroom. Relative status is primarily socially located around neighbors, friends, and fellow workers. Their perception is that an Anadolu school, even the lowest one, is relatively higher than any nonselective school. The relative distance between an Anadolu school graduate and a public middle-school graduate is perceived to be significant when viewed in the context of a family's class location. Their strategy is to locate a good public elementary school that can teach to the test. Perhaps in fifth grade, parents will send the child to an inexpensive lesson school a few months before the test.

At the other end of the spectrum, new middle-class families are more likely to spend what it takes to place a child in the highest possible rank of the private middle schools' hierarchy as measured by the test-taker's score. The attitude toward competition is best captured by a phrase in the argot of neoliberal culture: "Not winning is a going-out-of-business strategy." In other words, families adopt a do-or-die competitiveness toward winning the SMSEs that might be more appropriate to competing in financial markets.

Money matters in the competitive environment of the SMSEs because the cost of private market test services that are deemed necessary to win varies in quality and therefore cost. The market agent, or provider of expert services, that has the highest profile is the tutor. The press and parents frequently attribute the victory of winning one of the top schools to a tutor. This market also happens to be the least regulated market. In fact, it consists of unregistered, self-appointed "tutors." There is a yawning cavern between, say, neighbors or young university students who need pocket change and mature, experienced, self-educated tutors who enjoy the reputation for having developed techniques that annually land their fifth-grade test machines in the most desired private foreign schools.

In contrast, the market agent that meets the largest demand for expert services is the lesson school, which is licensed by the state. These are businesses located on commercial streets around the city that offer courses aimed directly at the SMSEs and that provide practice testing on a regular schedule. The reputation of lesson schools for helping parents achieve access to a good middle school varies. A small number are known for having students who routinely place students in the most desired private schools. The teachers at these lesson schools also tend to be licensed public school teachers moonlighting in order to increase their modest incomes. Parents vary in their knowledge of these schools, but even when they have the hard data they are likely to seek and accept the advice of persons in their own social network.

Agents of the market for expert test services generally are in common agreement that money is not the only form of capital and market agents are not the only form of expertise. One of the most redundant claims in interviews with market agents of whatever type is that none of their services can succeed without the total commitment of families, especially mothers. In other words, accumulated social and cultural

capital banked in families, when combined with families' economic capital, constitute the necessary conditions for winning the SMSEs.

Against the odds and facing imminent failure is a mother's belief that she can
manage the engineering of a test machine that will win the race. Time compres-
sion is the perception that every minute of preparation over a span of one year,
often extended to two years and beyond, and arguably inclusive of a private preschool in an early-childhood education plan, "counts" toward a higher test score
to the third decimal place. This belief, enunciated over and over in our interviews,
is the engine that creates the booming market for test services. Families that accepted the SMSEs as "necessary" while reviling the system as corrupt failed to
take into account the role that their own hypercompetitive attitude and practices
played in creating a high-end private market for test services. New middle-class
families do participate in their own making through the test preparation process,
but not as they would like. The demand for private market test services driven
by parents' test mania has led to high financial, social, and emotional costs for
the cultural reproduction of class privilege.

A quadrangular narrative provides further insights into the shape of the market based on family strategy and tactics. To explore the above claims in further
depth, the remainder of the chapter draws heavily on voices of the four agents
of test preparation: school/teacher, lesson school, tutor, and family. In order to
preserve the context that gives meaning to voices, we chose an interview from
each of the three market agents that is representative of the "best" practices of
its particular agency. The result is a characterization of the market at its expert
level of performance. The highest level of performance of the market is the level
of expertise most in demand by the most competitive families. These families are
savvy and willing to spend what is necessary to win. Frustration and anger enter
into strategy options that would appear "rational" because, we argue, there is no
single strategy or mix of services that can be shown to be better than others for
reasons we explore through the voices of parents toward the end of this chapter.

Voices of Market Agents

Given the communicative requirements of a market that makes education its
business, it is to be expected that their narratives reflect in part their self-interest
as defined by their location in the market for private school services. Private
schools can be expected to defend the values of classroom education while practicing those of the test for reasons of survival. Lesson schools can be expected
to defend the values of testing while promoting education from a narrower and
more pragmatic pedagogy. Tutors can be expected to take a narrow view of the
content of education and to focus exclusively on memory of content and technique to improve speed and accuracy to create a child test machine. Much of the
effort of agents of the market for test services aims at short cuts to winning by
reducing the importance of regular school classrooms. One common tactic that
some parents use in an overall strategy is to reduce the hours in regular schools
so as to increase the hours spent practicing for the test.

For particular cases it is expected that there would be a large variety of combinations of values and expectations, but this simplified framework will suffice to explore the connections between market segmentation of services and the rhetorical strategies of private schools, lesson schools, and tutors. We have chosen to focus on the discursive practices of three market agents, each typifying a subfield of the market for preparation services, one from each segment, in order to explore in depth their impact on parents' strategy options.

We want to know how agents of the industry differ among each other in their persuasive language and the extent to which rhetorical differences are related to their agency within the industry. While all have reservations about the state's construction of the system that structures the field of competitive relations, they all share a neoliberal ideology of education. They believe in the importance of the private sector of education and testing in general, but express their respective opinions about the problems and issues they pose for schooling and families. A case study approach allows us to locate different "voices" within the subfield of competitive market relations that make contrasting rhetorical claims to arrive at a multivocal understanding of expert market services from the point of view of its practitioners.

The industry has its own rhetorical strategies that differ according to subfields of competition: namely, private schools, lesson schools, and tutors. From the state's point of view, these constitute new "sectors" of the neoliberal national economy. There is competition between agents within each subfield, but here we concentrate on the subfields from the perspective of parents who struggle to put together a winning strategy based on their choice of schools and selection of combinations of market services.

As our primary informants, we selected experts who enjoy notoriety in Istanbul with regard to their particular subfields of expertise. For this exercise, we selected a private primary school owner and education administrator, a lesson school owner and business manager, and an independent tutor. All three were chosen not on the grounds of their typicality but rather on the grounds that they enjoyed very high reputations in their respective fields. They represent, as it were, the "best practices" of their respective agency and therefore can be expected to attract the most lucrative and competitive families' attention. All are highly knowledgeable and articulate about their sector and enjoyed success at the time of our research. We were also influenced in our selection by the clarity and power of their appeal, as well as an ability to make a persuasive case for their own practices. They are "active bearers of personal experience" (Williams 1973: 168–69) and express their own retrospective accounts of changes in education policies and practices during the liberalization period.

Faces of the Market for Education Services

Lale Ünal, Füsun Kuzuoğlu, and Vitali Meşulam are representative of the neoliberal up-market demand for SMSE test preparation services that were available by the mid-1990s. All three have education qualifications and years of experience in their respective endeavors.

Lale Ünal attended English Girls School before entering Boğaziçi University's Education Department in 1976. After encountering difficulties with the Ministry of National Education over opening an infant school, she was able to found Pinokyo Nursery School in 1980. In retrospect, she looks over the past fifteen years and marvels at how resistant the state was to the pedagogy and psychology of child development. To found her primary school, Yüzyıl Işıl, she had to form a group of partners and overcome bureaucratic obstacles that delayed the opening of the first stage until 1987. When Ünal took the next step of forming an investment group for the purpose of founding a middle school, she had yet more difficulty convincing the state bureaucracy that her experience and reputation qualified her.

According to Lale Ünal, Yüzyıl Işıl Primary School "attracts large numbers of children whose parents are university educated and are teachers and administrators in higher education, high-level state employees such as the diplomatic service, top managers of corporations and banks, and owners of their own businesses." She thought herself fortunate to have parents who were "opinion leaders" and "persons of cultural importance." Parents were attracted not only to her education philosophy—one might say, to her whole view of quality education—but also to a social class of people as much as to any particular classroom method or technique. Most parents find a school through social networks. The costs for sending a child to a new school like Yüzyıl Işıl are as high as those of the oldest elite, private foreign-language schools.

Füsun Kuzuoğlu went to middle school at private Kültür Lisesi in Ataköy and finished in the Atatürk Institute's English Department. After a career as a teacher for ten years at public Nilüfer Hatun Middle School, she became involved in the lesson school business through marriage to a son of the founders of FKM Lesson School. Her in-laws were retired schoolteachers who had founded YKM Lesson School in 1970. Their two sons took over the business in 1977 and changed the name to FKM, reflecting a business decision to prepare high school students to enter university examinations in physics, chemistry, and mathematics (the first letter of these subjects in Turkish gives the acronym FKM). Beginning in the 1980–81 teaching year, two years before the state instituted the national fifth-grade examinations, FKM offered fourth- and fifth-grade lessons. Over the years, the business expanded. Kuzuoğlu is now partner and manager of their new building in Mecidiyeköy. In addition to their preparation lessons for the SMSEs, they began to offer support courses, foreign language, repeat examinations, and university preparation lessons. But most importantly for this story, they opened up a research and development arm of their business to help parents with all aspects of managing their duties in preparing their child for the SMSEs. Their routinization of parent management was no small contribution to families who faced the fifth-grade year with fear and trepidation, not to mention bewilderment and ignorance.

FKM Lesson School takes several thousand students a year for the sole purpose of managing the test preparation process. Expansion is limited by a tradeoff between maintaining a strong "success rate" to attract parents and calculating the limits of efficient family management for profit. According to Kuzuoğlu, these limits have been reached and they have no plans for further expansion. FKM does not select the students who will come to FKM annually. She states flatly, "Those who come first to register will have places." This announcement is prompted by the common belief among parents that market agents in all sectors try to "cherry pick" students who make the agents look like experts.

Most parents find FKM by one of two routes. One is by word of mouth. Parents looking for lesson schools talk to other parents, friends, and neighbors. The other way to attract parents is more proactive. Kuzuoğlu "keeps up" with the Private Schools Association and with particular school administrators and their teachers. Where do FKM students come from? Kuzuoğlu is proud that: "Very few are from private primary schools. Of the one thousand students at the Mecidiyeköy campus, the parents of four hundred of them are university graduates; another two hundred have fathers with a university degree and mothers who have graduated from high school. Very few have parents who attained only primary school." The services FKM offers come in a package of lessons and test-taking skills for children, together with information and counseling services for parents. This range of quality services is reputed to be among the very best in the business. The cost is known to be "high," but includes a package of information relevant to making preferences about schools and counseling parents about the social and psychological problems that emerge in the home and how to manage them.

Vitali Meşulam has been tutoring for twenty-three years. After attending private middle school at Tarsus American College in the southeast of Turkey, he went to high school at Robert Lisesi before going on to Middle Eastern Technical University, where he earned both an undergraduate and graduate degree in chemical engineering. All of these schools emphasize English-language instruction. While at Middle Eastern in Ankara, he also entered the Education Department's six-semester-long Teaching Certificate Program. During graduate school, he taught chemistry at Ankara College for two years.

Meşulam's first encounter with tutoring was in Istanbul, where he had relocated with his family after finding work in a chemical corporation. When his neighbor, a cousin's daughter, was preparing to take middle school tests at a time before the introduction of the SMSE, her father solicited Meşulam's help. Each school had its own test. She won the test at Üsküdar Amerikan Lisesi, one of the top elite foreign-language schools. Meşulam's career in tutoring was launched. "Suddenly, I was working and giving lessons to relatives' and friends' children. Tutoring," he says, "has been a hobby, like some go to a bar for a drink or to play golf." He attributes part of his success to his training as a chemical engineer. Meşulam acknowledges that when he began tutoring, he was ignorant of the techniques and there really was no clear system and no simple way to acquire information. "For example, for the Robert examination, students were memorizing words from Mars comics—short or long words, without understanding the meaning." When the state introduced the SMSEs, Meşulam was forced to change his methods as well as reducing the number of his students.

Over time, his reputation grew as a tutor who repeatedly placed children in the top private foreign-language schools. Meşulam performs his daily tutoring after working at a chemical firm that produces chemical textile raw materials. He used to work there eight hours a day, but in 1996 he was working four hours, leaving most of his time for tutoring. Top tutors were earning untaxed income far in excess of income they could obtain from employment, even employment as a chemical engineer in a corporation.

Children come to Meşulam by word of mouth. Parents will telephone to make an appointment. Since demand for his services is high, parents find him, not vice versa, allowing him to decline appointments on multiple grounds of social affiliation or the state of a child's education performance to date. Depending on the outcome of a test he administers to chosen prospective students, Meşulam makes a selection. The reason he gives for "pretesting" as a selection mechanism is that his basic method of tutoring requires it. He gives lessons to pairs who are "equal" with one another. That way, he says: "they compete and are sure to do their homework. Some people say that I select only good students, but I am saying, 'the discipline is lacking in this child.'" After he accepts them: "if fifty children begin with me, forty-eight finish. That is very important because I hear, for example, that twenty of fifty children leave another group, then new ones come, others go. . . . I don't take any new students along the way after the preparation has begun."

Meşulam's "success rate" is extraordinary and his prices are reputed to be commensurate with his success. Significantly, perhaps, Meşulam offered no social and economic information about his clientele that would indicate their class status other than their ability to pay his up-market rates for technique. The tutor segment of the market has no organized public face. It tends to be more opaque to the public, less open in its operations than other segments. This opacity applies not only to information and finance but also to the "secrets" of technique. While all the parents we interviewed used the services of tutors, many complained loudly about their high costs. Media coverage of the SMSEs has raised the tutor to the rank of a neoliberal guru. In our family interviews, parents often expressed a surprising unfamiliarity with tutors' methods in contrast to their knowledge of elementary schools, school owners or administrators, and teachers. One reason may be that tutors have detached their expertise and distanced themselves from the more human social and emotional aspects of the preparation process, leaving these important dimensions of success or failure to school teachers and mothers.

Personalizing bureaucracy is a necessary activity in Turkish mundane social life (see chapter 5 on social networks as social capital). The subfield of test preparation is no exception. Parents increasingly attributed success to that last little bit of superior technique held by the master tutor. They recognized the value of other agents and their methods, but the relentless pressure of winning led to a collective belief in the marginal utility of the tutor's focus on fine-tuned technique. This belief is not surprising, since the preparation process was basically an interpersonal one that linked individual service providers personally to a mother manager who would ultimately bear the burden or enjoy the pride of the final outcome.

The belief in marginal utility was expressed in the folklore of the test in such expressions as "to the third decimal point," an allusion to the way in which the SMSEs are scored. The level of competition has reached a state such that it requires the third decimal point between adjacent scores to determine who will be offered the last seat in the selection process of a preferred school. A test-taker can be eliminated from a school's cadre of students by .001 points. Another folkloric expression is "one question, one test." This alludes to the same idea of intense competition to the point where one wrong answer eliminates a test-taker from entering the cadre of a preferred school. Yet another folkloric icon of the SMSEs is the commonly heard statement that appears in narratives as "ten students had perfect scores." The astonishment that accompanies this phrase emanates from a shared belief that the number of student test machines tuned to perfection is rising at an alarming rate, increasing the pressure on every family to "do more" for the child. The draconian practice of the state to raise the difficulty of the test to avoid replication of scores has fallen behind the ability of market agents to prepare students to win. For parents, ten students with perfect scores (no mistakes) indicates that nine students who otherwise would have been admitted to Robert Lisesi will have to go to another school, and so on down the selection system.

From the standpoint of parents, schools can be compared but tutors cannot. Add to this the opaqueness of tutors' techniques, and parents are faced with strategy options that are difficult to make and even more difficult to assess. Parents' generalized belief in the marginal value of an agent is a subjective assessment after the fact and becomes a topic of endless conversation. In other words, there is no one best way to prepare a student for the SMSEs. One might argue that the outcome, the score, is a sharp measure of strategy options, but no part of the system can calculate or measure the aptitude of the student and the importance of the family habitus as a contribution to cultural reproduction by means of social capital. We return to this issue below when we explore the market for test services from the perspective of parents' strategy options and their own experience of creating a strategy. Parents we interviewed generally use the services of all the market agents in varying degrees but rely on social networks and personal values.

Rhetorical Discourses of Idealism, Pragmatism, and Technique

To hear Lale Ünal, Füsun Kuzuoğlu, and Vitali Meşulam talk about themselves and their practices is to be convinced as a parent of the need for their services. Their persuasive talk is framed by the logic of the hegemonic state's *objektif sistem* and its discourse of numbers and the one best answer. As market agents for preparation services, however, their discourse is framed by their competitive niche in the market and aimed at appealing to the aspirations, fears, and anxieties of families who are their clients. Their discourses are rhetorical as well as referential, relying on persuasion as much as appeal to objective expertise. They have in common the good fortune to have as their clients new middle-class families of sufficient means to pay the highest prices for education services that reduce the risk of failure to a minimum.

Because parents are so concerned about the marginal value of one extra service that might tip the scale in their direction, or the fear of failing if they haven't taken advantage of every possible service, they believe that they must work closely with competing agents for their children to succeed. Industry rhetoric provides a window on family experience of the system. Agents in different segments of the market have their own rhetorical voices, but they also share a common rhetoric about the value of their services against, say, the elementary schools that teach only education, not testing. Nontesting, progressive elementary schools embrace the rhetoric that each child is different, that the subject matter of courses will influence children's lives, and that education is part of a larger philosophy of child development. Schoolteachers remain with their students through the first five years of education. To hear them speak, they remember each child with respect and adults remember their elementary school teacher with great fondness. From the founding of the republic, women employed by the state were encouraged to enter the teaching profession as a mission and obligation to modernize the nation. To this day, many schoolteachers view themselves as being on a mission to protect the foundations of the republic.

By contrasting rhetorical voices of persons whose business it is to help parents prepare their children for the SMSEs, which looms over and dominates every other desire, we gain a clear insight into the partnership between state and market in the maintenance of social class in Turkey. The rhetoric of market agency articulates the intersection of state, market, and family in a field of competitors designed to reproduce class with an expertise and precision that is difficult for parents to express.

In areas where they are at their greatest distance within the education industry, Lale Ünal's voice is the rhetoric of progressive education turned idealist in a state bureaucracy perceived by her to be the domain of education philistines. With a firm grasp on the necessities, her rhetoric is subversive of the system, choosing a strategy of resistance to state domination by working within the system to subvert it.

Vitali Meşulam, in contrast, not only has accepted the test system but also has embraced its inner logic and language. He is wholly inside the system in his own education, his predisposition toward technical solutions, and his fascination with testing. His voice is the rhetoric of engineering solutions with numbers in an education system he perceives to be, to borrow a phrase from Jacques Ellul, "absolute technique" (1964). Meşulam appears to have undergone a transformation from the disposition of a chemical engineer to that of a test engineer who can solve the purely technical problems of barriers to success that parents face as a result of the imposition of the SMSEs. But to do so, his rhetorical claims must succeed in reducing the examination process to its elemental function of obtaining the highest score in the most technically efficient way. He does not concern himself with the knowledge of the content of different subject matters, only with techniques that will help a student identify and select the right answer out of four options to a question designed for that task on a test.

Füsun Kuzuoğlu's rhetoric is closest to the pragmatic voice adopted by those who find business solutions to "exam success" through discipline, organization, and accurate market information on all aspects of the preparation process. She sees her primary service to be counseling parents about the probabilities at various levels of failure up to success and how to plan for an outcome. Her services and those of other members of her team bridge the divide between those of Lale Ünal and Vitali Meşulam. Her rhetoric is an appeal to parents that ultimately rests on the social psychology of child development. But her main concern is to translate information useful to families' education plans from school preferences through the long preparation period to school selection after the test results are in. Relative to Meşulam, technique is one small but important part of the process restricted to the testing classes offered by FKM. Her rhetoric is a controlled attempt to serve high ideals of quality tempered by the realism of her corner of the market for preparation services.

The Rhetoric of Pedagogical Idealism

Lale Ünal's appeal to the new middle-class ideology of market freedom and individual enterprise is a "vision" of children's education that attributes to children many of the characteristics that neoliberal ideology grants to adults. In this sense she is an exemplar of the neoliberal discourse appropriate to the liberalization episode in general, and in particular to the field of education. The force of her rhetoric, however, derives not merely from ideological commitment to child education but also from her personal experiences of doing battle with the state education bureaucracy for the right to have her own school and to preach a subversive doctrine of children's rights. The whole point of her rhetoric is that, in Turkey, children's rights are being subverted by state-centered education policy that ignores the cognitive and emotional development of eleven-year olds. Her personal experience traces the arc of changes in state education policy and ideology since 1980.

According to Ünal, in the last ten to fifteen years there has been a significant change in MEB (Ministry of National Education) bureaucrats' and technocrats' belief in private education, their trust in it and the necessity for it. In her words: "an 80 to 90 percent change. But some of this is exaggerated. At this moment, 1.3 to 1.5 percent of schools in Turkey are private. People can't choose when they have no service to choose from. You can't say there is no need for private education. It's necessary to create order, to encourage healthy qualities, trust, and utility. Private schooling is able to attain these goals; only it isn't encouraged by the state."

This brings Ünal to her vision of primary education, the administration of her own school, and the middle school examinations. She begins with the latter and moves toward her education philosophy:

> In Turkey you're very well aware there is a fifth-grade fact; in our schools we don't manage the orderliness of primary school very effectively. There is a thing, a dinosaur, which manages us. To do well submitting to it, to do badly submitting to it, to revolt against it—nothing matters. To found a primary school is to accept it. This dinosaur, this fact, about this much we will not be able to make a decision. This is a "fact." It is necessary to accept this because in Turkey there is an enduring education system. Turkey is not a rich country. Turkey will not be able to give a quality education to all the children who want one. I very much believe what I have said. We are very unaccustomed to paying for education with the culture we have carried over from the Ottomans.

The "fact," the "dinosaur," is, of course, the SMSEs. But in her rhetoric she is not inside the system logic; she is outside it, accepting it only in order to work around the edges, to get "respect" back for private education:

> In Turkey, private education associations weren't very respected, with the exception of one or two foundations that became state schools. One could receive a diploma without satisfying parents or clients. Foundations accepted students with other understandings. Private education was wanting in quality and didn't develop in content. The state didn't invest sufficiently in education while at the same time protecting its prerogatives against attempts by the private sector to invest.

The result, Ünal points out, is that "it is necessary that you become more selective as you go because it is impossible to give an education with content and quality in a country in which half of the state's population is youth and there is not the corresponding growth in the education sector." In such conditions, she explains her own education foundation and contrasts it with that of the state's foundation:

> How am I looking at this examination as an education administrator? If the SMSEs is a fact, then it is a very rational matter. Whatever will be, will be. But you work to maximize the payday in the least harmful way for every child who enters the SMSEs. In this school, we are in a position to build on this proposition. We're questioning the education foundation in order that every child reaches a level that is correct for that child to attain its maximum productivity in given conditions. It's a child's right to primary education free from anxiety. We as professionals have a responsibility to complain about changes in macroinstitutions that we don't want in our school. Let's say in summarizing that these are the foundations of my education administration.

Her aim in primary education is to recognize the SMSEs as a fact but to minimize the overall effect on every child by ensuring continuation of quality education. The new private schools like hers can have their cake and eat it too. If her fifth-graders do not win the test, at least they can continue on in schools like hers, solving parents anxiety about where to find quality education. This is an allusion to the common understanding in Turkey today that primary-school classrooms are either too overcrowded to achieve any goals aimed at individual development or are aimed specifically at winning the test, sacrificing classroom content to test technique, and creating great anxiety in the process.

Ünal is frustrated about the SMSE system because it works against her vision of a society that will grant to every child the right to attain his or her full education potential rather than one in which 90 percent of children will be judged "failures" by a test on one day at the end of primary school. One of the foundations of her pedagogy in the Turkish context is to recognize that many children are fearful of the SMSEs. She uses the metaphor of the collapse of a dam to describe how children form a psychological reaction to "doping" during preparation. Her own way to "maximize payday" while minimizing harm is to begin to observe children by third grade, tightening the requirements of testing by fourth grade, so that by fifth grade, parents and students have a level of "comfort" about how they will approach the examination or be able to avoid it altogether. Children who are prepared for it can be encouraged to meet their level of competition, others can be encouraged to enter the examinations because "it may make them feel better," and still others not to enter it but to remain in privates schools like hers. "Talking to parents this way and being in a position to provide a quality alternative has met with a good response."

The Rhetoric of Pragmatism

In Füsun Kuzuoğlu's narrative, there is an underlying theme of focusing on and stabilizing the family as the unit under pressure during the SMSE preparation process. The narrative begins with a story of SMSE mania that lies at the heart of FKM's success story and moves toward "principles" that frame a contract with parents. The story begins with ratcheting up test scores:

> Students are getting better and better at the exam, scores are higher and higher, and the exam is getting tougher. The increasing intensity of competition is forcing parents to begin earlier and earlier. The result is that parents want FKM services earlier. At the end of every year since 1980 there has been an increase in the scores of those preparing for the examination. I remember from examination results in the 1980s. In 1985, when a child was able to score 100 points, the best performance in Turkey was 86 to 87 net points. In contrast, there were twenty-nine perfect scores in 1993. Of course, this is connected with the difficulty of the examination. But for every year since 1980, the score of students is higher because people are not waiting until fourth and fifth grade to prepare.

There is pressure to begin preparation earlier. The increase in the intensity of competition is only partly explained by the increase in numbers taking the examination. There also is a cultural dynamic at work, one that is located in the competitiveness of new middle-class children of families imbued with a neoliberal spirit of accumulation. By her own reckoning, 40 percent of FKM's clientele may include some of these families:

> There is a group preparing from first grade. Many people are saying, "Are you developing a first-grade program for us?" If we open a course for third-graders, I believe that people would come in great numbers. But we don't find correct the view that being a mother is like being an educator. If a child is receiving a good foundation from the mother in the first three years, then it will be at a point where it can attain greater things. Preparing from first grade is a little exaggerated.

Much of FKM's rhetoric concerns the worries and anxieties of parents and children toward the whole process, a recognition of their apprehension, and an attempt to meet those needs. As a result, they have turned themselves into a counseling center as much as a lesson school, filling in the gaps between what goes on at home, in the primary school classroom, and at the tutor's. In other words, there is a transposition of the family as well as the test-taker and FKM has created services of value to help families create a test environment for the test-taker.

FKM has chosen the strategy of entering into a form of social contract with families of test-takers. Kuzuoğlu rhetorically suggests that there is a need to counsel parents about themselves and their relation with their child in a social atmosphere. She believes that FKM is successful because of "principles" that she attaches to a contract with parents that is remarkable for its forthrightness and clarity: "The most important thing is our clear principles. After this, it is to make money, but first in order is not that. We actually wouldn't make money if we gave first importance to it." These principles are a combination of published guidelines, suggestions, and rules of thumb FKM has evolved for how to counsel parents through the preparation process while providing lessons for the child. When parents choose FKM, they choose the whole package of services included in the price.

Lale Ünal's rhetoric is not independent of her organization and its goals. Her clients are interested in a long-term relationship, probably at least five years of primary school, but prospectively from kindergarten or first grade right straight through high school. She built spaces for parents to be present in her school at any time of the day as she has the children all day, five days a week. Her rhetoric encompasses more of their children's lives than could be expected either from the more circumscribed social spaces and functions of Füsun Kuzuoğlu's organization or Vitali Meşulam's home enterprise. FKM keeps children for the short-term, sometimes as short as half a year, at most two years, although Kuzuoğlu indicates that the escalation of competition within the middle class had reached the point where there is demand for lessons even at the first-grade level. Children appear only twice a week, mostly after school, in the evenings, or on weekends—i.e., an interstitial routine in a weekly schedule governed by others. Parents drop children off at the lesson house and return to pick them up. At various points during the annual cycle, parents come to meetings, teacher-parent conferences, or appear for private counseling. FKM simply did not enjoy the degree of control that comes from continuous association among mother, tutor, and child, nor did it control the selection of students to the same degree that Meşulam did, nor did the lesson house engender the same loyalty and trust of its clientele as that enjoyed by Ünal. The foundation of FKM's rhetoric was about specific pragmatic principles attached to a contract, not a generalized vision of child education institutionalized in a school. Its booklets and counseling service represented a compromise for middle-class parents between Ünal's pedagogy of education and Meşulam's technique for testing.

The qualifications of FKM's partners go well beyond business management and administration to include child teaching, psychology, and social delinquency. Their combined expertise, along with good marketing, was apparent in booklets produced by their Guidance and Psychological Counseling Services Unit on a variety of topics that together comprise a sophisticated approach to education services. Their target group was mixed new middle and middle-class parents. There are at least seven such booklets, most of which concern topics about parent-child communications in the context of the examinations. Parents who sign contracts receive these booklets as well as attend meetings and counseling sessions at which they learn more about their content.

The Rhetoric of Technique

Vitali Meşulam is after results. Neither the findings of child development on early education nor the psychosocial communicative dynamics of parent-child interactions are of much concern to him. Literally, he is an engineer and, figuratively, he sees himself as engineering test success by increasing speed and accuracy in answering questions. Meşulam comes the closest of our three representative cases of SMSE services to the view that the system is about technique, that technique measures intelligence, that children can become test machines, and that Turkish society benefits from the state's objective gatekeeping over access to the best schools:

> When I meet the parents, they are saying like this, "let's meet our obligations to our children." They say this with intensity. For example, they say, "let the lessons be taken. The child will blame us later, so let us make them be taken." They want to say, "we performed our duty."

All the people we interviewed offered the opinion that "Turkish people are serious about education." Furthermore, they view education as a family obligation. But finding an occupation for a child also is a family matter, and just as often so is finding a spouse and ensuring that a married couple has a home complete with furnishings. These are all obligations of the family, and families are serious in their obligations. Meşulam explained that "families are doing their duty" by entering their children in the SMSEs. When it comes to the family, he is concerned specifically with his own method for making test machines in the context of a family's duty. Over the years, he explained, he has gotten hold of the system sufficiently to provide only twenty-four lessons, each one-and-a-half hours in length. But he has to explain to parents their duty:

> It's an important matter. Now, I myself give my personal program laden with homework. If the child does the homework I'm giving over and above the one-and-a-half hour lesson . . . actually, it is impossible to do this in less than ten hours for every hour of lesson. Those books are very difficult because, although they are not like the old ones with twelve hundred pages, they are between nine hundred and a thousand pages. Eh, children forget. Now, at the time I'm making a test at the end of the fourth grade, 35 percent of the children were average in social science. When thinking about this fourth-grade subject in fifth grade, it becomes impossible because there also are fifth-grade subjects. For this reason, I apportion all the work over one year. This requires a lot of homework.

Meşulam is aware of the burden he places on a family, but he is involved in its affairs only peripherally. In his system of paired tutorials, a child will have the homework complete because she or he is competing with another child. Mothers importune him, but there is little he can say. His program requires it and he can say "with absolute certainty" that the child cannot succeed without ten hours of memorization for every hour of a social studies lesson, not to mention other lessons. In this case, his rhetorical claim is a simple one: lesson to homework ratios succeed because the work required is memorization of facts within the framework of test-taking technique. His lesson provides the test-taking technique and drill of answering a multiple-choice question with speed and accuracy, the homework provides material and recall. His program has withstood the test of time. Meşulam makes no rhetorical claims about the rights of children nor does he claim that individual children differ, except in one respect. When he first tests them before accepting them, he tries to pair them according to their "equality," which means a willingness to complete heavy loads of homework and submit to his "discipline." He says as a matter of fact, "I want to control absolutely the homework when doing lessons."

When Meşulam talks about how parents and children deal with failure, he credits neither the mother nor child with suffering from any lasting effects of their ordeal. Instead, he is inclined to believe that some children don't improve because they don't compete, and they don't compete because their parents don't exert themselves. His method involves treating "cases on the same level." In addition, there is "slack in the system." As schools drop their base points to fill their contingents during the period after the SMSEs when the schools begin their selection process, he believes that most of those who really know they competed will have choices. When they finally are selected and make their commitment— that is, when they buy their uniform—there is a psychology of success. According to Meşulam: "they will declare victory—'I have won.' Finally, the system has also improved on this score because there were many more Anadolu schools and private schools in 1995 than there were in 1984. A family that makes the effort is likely to get into an Anadolu school or private Turkish school."

The real force of Meşulam's rhetoric lies in his discourse of numbers. Whatever the topic, he adverts to hypothetical examples of number scenarios. He is fascinated by the test as a game that is being perfected through his agency and others like him. He not only accepts the system and works to perfect it, he enthusiastically embraces the system and is fascinated by it. His melding with the system appears in many contexts, for example, when he talks about how well the system works as a mechanism of selectivity:

> There also is a question about the differences between the three hundred thousand students who take the exam and the three thousand who are serious. Let's say there are two thousand students who score between 90 and 100. Let's say also perhaps one to two thousand who score below 20. Others are in between. There are one hundred questions, each worth one point. You are saying, "in one mistake is one point and loss of one school." Those points, of course, are also groups. For each wrong question, many fall, perhaps three to four thousand. I know by counting how many standard deviations. Very interesting, very, very interesting, this system. Of course, injustice, there is something absent, I don't know. I don't think about a better system. Because it can't be. How could it be? You are doing an exam, there isn't another remedy.

Impatient with families who proclaim the system to be unjust, Meşulam responds that there is no "remedy" to this problem, just the system itself. He offers a technical solution for what he believes to be a technical problem. He stops short of suggesting that the exam system is part of a larger politics of education. His view contrasts with that of Lale Ünal, who made her rhetorical appeal for giving respect to private education not only on moral grounds but also on grounds that the state public education system would not be rich enough in the foreseeable future to support all those who want a quality education. The sheer weight of numbers—nearly half the population of Turkey is under fifteen years of age—buries state public education under a heavy burden from which it has not been able to dig out. Ünal levels her accusation at a national assembly that has pandered to a populist politics of education expansion over three decades without appropriating sufficient funds for education expenditures that would make quality education a reality for a broad middle class. She views the bureaucratic response of an efficient selection-out system to be a travesty on the middle class. Ünal would find many supporters among the families we interviewed. Meşulam's clearer if simpler vision is that the SMSEs represent a more objective, efficient mechanism of selectivity and that its selection-out strategy is "a good thing for Turkey." For him, a more "efficient" system is also a more just system.

Voices of Parents

In our interviews with persons in different structural positions in the field of competitive social relations, we discovered a high degree of agreement among all agents about its rules, regulations, and reasons for existing. Each agent, however, viewed the field from a different perspective depending on his or her own interest as well as the interest of clients. In order to understand the practices of agents that provide market services and families that plan their children's preparation for the SMSEs, we needed to explore the "whole set of strategies pursued by the agents" operating in a capitalist market for education services (Waquant 1991: 57–58). These are the agents that together reproduce the cultural capital of the new middle class in the field of education. What is obvious from our interviews is that parents differ in their determination to win, in their cohesion, in their ability to put together a coherent strategy, in their material resources, and in the pressures they face in their daily lives. Children differ in their maturity, their aptitude for one subject area over another, and their degree of resistance to the test. All of these factors interact with each other in complex ways that make it difficult to predict a winning strategy independently of its family context. It is less difficult to make an educated guess about a losing strategy.

Excerpts from two contrasting interviews contextualize some of the common problems that confront parents and help to put a human face on strategy options. Strategy options are packaged, requiring forethought that includes the following: (1) choice of elementary schools (public or private, particular named schools); (2) mix of market services (lesson school and tutor, lesson school, tutor, tutor for each subject); (3) cost; (4) support services such as psychological help.

In Search of a Winning Strategy

Our interview with Meltem and Arda took place one weekend afternoon in their comfortable, modern apartment in Fenerbahçe, an upper middle-class district on the Asian side of Istanbul along the eastern shore of the Sea of Marmara, where local residents enjoy bike riding, running, and strolling. Meltem and Arda have two children, an older son Taylan and a daughter Canan who is preparing for the SMSEs. Their apartment is close to the private Kalamış School where Canan is enrolled and near to the Galatasaray Club on a small peninsula jutting out into the sea. Arda's family has membership at the club where the whole family enjoys sports activities.

Abbreviation of names: wife is Meltem (M); husband is Arda (A). Interview was conducted in Turkish and translated into English.

M: Of course, what I wished for my son was Alman Lisesi [German High School]. Because they teach two languages and he is a boy. However, my son's teacher was a little weak. My son had no fault. And I could not realize this because he was my first child. He could not get a good background. After that . . . starting in the fourth [grade] is a little late.

M: [After he took the test] his score allowed him to get into an Anadolu school [Hüseyin Avni Sözen]. But we said, "Since we started this whole business for [winning] private schools . . . and so we did not enroll him there. We enrolled him in Saint Benoit.

M: I learned like this. I looked around. I learned that everybody is like crazy. That is, everybody used to say, "I don't make my child do anything. He is only going to one private teacher. But, thank God, this was good. He got in Robert." I learned that these were not true. I learned that the mothers compete more than the children. The private teachers prepare the children the way mothers want them to. That is, the children actually don't know anything. To ask, "which school will be better?" It turned out that the mothers choose the schools. I saw that [they] study with not one but several teachers. Nobody has one private teacher anymore; they tend to go to teachers that specialize in teaching a certain subject. For science, a science teacher; for social sciences, a social sciences teacher; for Turkish literature, a Turkish literature teacher; they get a teacher for each subject. I see that the way to succeed got harder. I think that it is a matter of resources.

A: The education you're going to give to a child is related to the child's capacity. My two children are different. You try to work on the one you think has the potential. My daughter is like that. But our first child, my son, lived through our experience. Now we are using our experience to raise the levels of our daughter. For private foreign-language schools, we have this Mr. Ergüder. If it's up to my wife, we need another teacher or a *kurs* [lesson school]. Now, this is such a hard thing. . . . Believe me. . . . You are in between two lines. Is only Mr. Ergüder enough? We want Robert, emotionally. . . . After that, should we send her to *kurs*? And education teachers, *kurs* [lesson teachers in groups of two, three, or four] are more subject based. Not test based. Evaluations are limited. Then there are *kurslar* such as FKM and others. These are totally test based. I mean, they make the child solve hundreds, even thousands, of [test] questions all through the year. Thus, if the term fits here, the children become "question bastards." Should we add this, too? Because if you're getting into a race, you should play the game by its rules. If this kid can be improved and if the other kids who are below [this kid's level] can go above [his or her level] with a lot of studying, then you have to move one step up to recover that capacity. Now I am in a dilemma.

M: When I took Canan [our daughter] to this school, the aim of this school was to have different . . . lesson teachers and to have them teach one on one and for the child to have a relaxed year with no homework. Moreover, Mr. Hikmet gives names because others like Mr. Ergüder, and Mr. Erkar [well-known for improving techniques that can increase test speed and accuracy] can't prepare [children] for middle-school tests. Because it is not their branch. A teacher can't be successful in every subject. Mr. Hikmet is good in Turkish, Ms. Fatma is good in math, etc.

The other day we were talking: "should we do that? Should we go to this teacher?" and so on. Canan had taken the trial exam offered by Istanbul Erkek Lisesi [a prominent public school]. Two thousand something students took the exam. Canan's [results] were worse than we had expected. She was 420th, but she should have been in the first 5 percent. Of course, I was very sad. "Why did this happen? There's something wrong. It's because of the school," etc.

M: In these conditions, if nothing comes from Allah, if she does not get sick that day, I think Canan has the capacity to get into a French school. But my reason to prepare her by taking her to Mr. Ergüder is maybe she will make it to Üsküdar [American School]. Actually, I want that.

The reason for me to get involved in this race is for my child to be able to go to a private school. But not only for her to learn a new language, for her to go to a private school that provides a foreign education. Otherwise, you know, there are some schools in Turkey, private schools. But [they are] private Turkish schools. Frankly, I don't want her to go to a private Turkish school. Because I want her to get the education of the school she goes to fully. I want it [the education] to be in their [the private schools'] style. For this reason, for her to learn a foreign language, and for her to be able to get something out of them [the private school], I prefer that she go to a foreign private school.

A: As soon as a teacher makes known of his or her students who get into a middle school, he or she becomes distinguished. Of course, whoever is in this business would have researched teachers. You see, there are so many crooked things in this event. Today, all [private] teachers accept students as a result of an exam, all teachers. Be careful, this is very important. They accept students of a certain level. For example, they ask fifty questions and do not accept students who make seven mistakes out of fifty answers. Now, if we look back and think, what is the [real] quality of the teacher? If my child has *nüve*, this child will reach a certain level with support, anyway. Of course, the real aim [of the teachers] is to be able to make a name to make money. If you accept children of a certain level, teach them some things and so if they get to wherever they want, then I'll make a name and so there'll be demand [for my services]. If I can bring a child with fifty mistakes down to twenty mistakes to such a level, then I am successful. I don't think any of the teachers today are successful.

Money

A: What happens? As these names appear, "he got five children into [middle school]," "Ten children into . . . " This is a matter of supply-demand. Commercial, it is commercial: receipt-free commerce, tax-free commerce. "We work from morning 'til evening"—excuse me, like, whatever. We are of the group that pays taxes to the government. The child is going to have two days of stress. One day he will take the private schools' test, and on another day he will take the Anadolu School test. What is this? The child is going to have two days of stress. One day he will take the private schools' test, and on another day he will take the Anadolu school test. Until that time you are locked to him [the teacher] and you have to be a slave. "Oh, as long as he pays attention to my child. . . ." That's how it is. Thus, I am going back [to what I was saying]. The families, us, created this crooked system. It's totally like this and the families that create it are of a certain economical status. If you look into this, they are very pitiful. Believe me, they are very pitiful. In public schools [in one classroom] there are seventy to eighty students. The ones that sit at the very back have no chance of learning. As long as this injustice of education in Turkey continues like this, the dimensions [number] of private schools . . . I'm not against private schools. But I am totally against private teachers earning money at such high levels. I don't have money; I can't make use of these opportunities of the government [access to private education through the SMSE]. You have money, your child is going to get the best education. There is no such thing! This cannot be justified by free economy or logic. . . . It doesn't make sense to the heart or the mind. But it is an order [system]. It's not us, but the ones above who should correct this. For some reason, none of the ministers of education tried to fix this education up until now. Of course, this also has economical reasons. . . . the pressure from private schools.

There used to be an upper price limit from the beginning. They [the private schools] went above it. Therefore, [now] the price goes up to wherever it can. Therefore today there are private primary schools with tuitions up to [$2,500] annually without including the payments for private teachers. Then there's another thing: "For what school are you preparing your child?" "For Robert?" "What about you?" Nobody is getting prepared for Alman Lisesi, Avusturya, Saint Benoit, etc. Everybody prepares for Robert. We are getting prepared for Robert, I mean, the total expenses of a family going for Robert, for 1996, is not less than [$10,000].

A Winning Strategy

Our interview with Zuhal and Ata took place in the comfortable salon of their spacious new apartment located in Ulus, a fashionable, new middle-class district of Istanbul in proximity to Boğaziçi University, international hotels the fashionable

Akmerkez Mall with designer labels in the upscale residential developments in Levent, and the even more recent Kanyon shopping complex in Maslak where the new Istanbul Stock Exchange attracts hotels, restaurants, and related business services.

In a three-hour taped interview, our questions ranged across all aspects of the SMSEs and related issues in education. What follows are excerpts of those parts of the interview that include a strategy for winning interspersed with commentary related to the market for education services.

Abbreviation of names: the wife is Zuhal (Z); her sister is Fatma (F); Zuhal's daugher is Esra (E); Fatma's daughter is Ulya (U); Zuhal's husband is Ata (A). Interview was done in Turkish and translated into English.

Z: I entered this race because I graduated from a private foreign school, which means Esra's growing environment was very important; her friends and her education were going to affect her future.

A: Because of the pressure from outside, you know, because of the social pressure, it was a must [to register for the private SMSEs] for the purpose of [acquiring a foreign] language.

F: Until Ulya was in the fourth grade, I did not worry about entering her in this race and in a private foreign school. But I, also, am a graduate of a private foreign school and during my life this brought me many advantages. I benefited in my work and social life. By coincidence, at the end of fourth grade, Ulya entered a test given by a very famous teacher. She scored higher than the other kids even though she, unlike the others, had no special preparation or tutoring. I thought I was being unfair to her, that's why I entered her in the race.

Z: We did not have to learn anything about the race we did not know before. People go into this race by knowing what's involved. When people look from the outside they think it is easy. As you get involved, you find out about the stress that's involved, finding out as you go along.

F: Esra and Ulya took the Anadolu school and private SMSE and were accepted into them. Sometimes students take an exam because the teacher wants it. We preferred the *kolejler* [private foreign schools]. We only wanted the *kolejler* and their first choice was what they got.

Z: The two systems are different. In the Anadolu school system, there are a lot of little bureaucratic things you have to do. You register [school preferences] before the SMSEs, they want your choice list. Five, I think, this year, three the year we took the exam. If the [test] points you received matched one of the [school] choices on your list you would be eligible for that school. If not, you are exposed. With the *kolejler*, it is not like that. You go take the SMSEs, you receive the scores and then you choose what ever [school] fits you best. The *kolejler* have this advantage.

A: What we have to learn from this system, it is a test. [Elementary] schools don't teach this system. [They] only teach information. During this race, a problem-solving system is important, learn this with their test tutors, those private teachers, All the preparation is towards this goal. The ability of solving the test is what makes the kid get a good score or not.

F: My interpretation is different. I realized after I got involved, I realized the system was based on memorizing, including math, I believe, which is supposed to be different—but even math, at the end, after solving for so long, repeating the same problems. More than math, science and social matters—I believe that science and social science requires forming opinions and judgments. If a child studies math well, she can solve thirty out of thirty problems, that's what I believe. In math, you don't need to be smart; in social science and science, the differences between children have to do with opinions. That is where you see the differences between children and their test scores.

Z: It [preparation] all happened at our home. It was what I requested. Normally, in general, in the group, they all end at a different time. I did not want Esra to lose time on the road, never wanted her to lose time. Also, Esra gained a lot because the tutor can show up at 4 pm instead of 2 pm. And if you spend an hour on the road for nothing, you end up losing three hours. We never lost time.

Z: My first step in preparing Esra for the race was finding her well-known tutors. Two hours with each tutor. In addition, math and social science, science, these subjects were rotated on a regular basis. She also was going to a regular school but we were not very attached to that school because they were doing nothing. I was focusing on Esra twenty-four hours a day. Besides school, we always did tests, new tests; we got every test in the market that year, from other tutoring places, private tutoring centers—all the tests I gathered and worked with Esra at home. We studied together, all year we devoted ourselves to studying and preparing.

F: At fourth grade, Ulya attended a general tutoring center twice a week. In addition to this group class, I helped her with her math. We did everything in fifth grade, gathering tests from the market, like everybody else was doing, so that the child doesn't forget. Ulya did attend the famous course at Istanbul Erkek Lisesi in fourth grade but not in fifth grade.

F: The group lessons are important. Some children have personal lessons; others have group sessions. When there are more people, there is competition to learn that lesson. It really helps. Ulya, my daughter, started out in a three-person group. There was a friend named Pelin in that group. This child was preparing herself to become number one in Turkey. She was super. She was better than my daughter. The other girl was Belma. Because I was from Robert, Mr. Rıdvan [the tutor] took her into this group. We weren't as sure of Ulya as we were of the others. The teacher did not have much belief in Ulya. She never got the good grades like Pelin and Belma. I mean, if they received 99 or 98, my child got 88 or 89. It wasn't bad. One day Pelin asked her what her choice was. Ulya said that she wanted Robert Lisesi as her first choice. Then Pelin laughed and said, "You and Robert is not a match." This hurt my child so much that she doubled her studying. She studied to be better than Pelin. This was the power of being in a group that caused her to really study. She would not have been able to do it alone. This was the best motivation. After the private SMSEs, when Pelin was chosen second and my daughter was in first place [in the nation], she was so happy. Group study is very important.

F: Mr. Rıdvan generally takes new students. All the other teachers have assessment tests before they take children. So they accept any child that scores 75 and over. If the child can get a 75, then she has the capacity to win the SMSEs. The teacher only takes the children with the capacity to be successful. The teacher must also keep her reputation. That is why they choose the good students. In the following year, parents will want to know how many of the teacher's students entered Robert, how many entered Üsküdar, how many entered the Alman Lisesi. Parents hear about this and go to the right teacher.

Z: Mr. Rıdvan eliminates students over a few months, after giving all of them a chance.

F: There are private elementary schools that tutor children for the SMSEs, but I don't believe in them. There is a school called Yüzyıl Işıl. They have class all day. The school has its own tests. I tried some of them at home. All the children have three to five teachers. The school does really well. I do not know if it is because of the teachers. The school is really nice. I am sure that the students learn something, but I do not believe that it is from the teacher because both Esra and Ulya both experienced the same thing. Zero.

Z: There is a school in Bursa [across the Sea of Marmara, two hours by automobile]. They give lessons all day on Saturdays and Sundays. It is the only school that prepares children for the SMSEs. They really prepare the children well and have at least ten children enter Robert every year.

U: At least ten. I am sure there are more. Most of the children who board at Robert, ten to fifteen students, come from there. My best friend [at Robert] came from there. Attending the Saturday and Sunday SMSE course was mandatory.

F: The school in Bursa is a very competitive school and prepares the children very well. If you ask, would I send my children there, I would not. It is like a Nazi camp. It really is [pause] Saturdays and Sundays for five years, beginning in first grade. I am against having no childhood [pause] seven days a week. There are strict rules and you have to obey them.

U: When I think about it now, I see that I was pushed. During that time, everywhere, including in my dreams, I saw tests. I go to bed, I get up—I see tests. Even though I had very good grades in the tests, I did not even study for the Anadolu school tests. During that time I watched TV when I came home. Watching one or two hours of TV was a big deal at that time, I felt like I let it go. But after I finished fifth grade, I told my mom, "I wish I could go through that time again, it did not really bother me." Maybe this is because I ended up at a very good school [Robert Lisesi]. To see the positive results of all my hard work, it was a big prize. That's why I said it did not bother me, but I guess if I was not very successful at the end it may have been different then.

E: I also agree with Ulya. I was very bored in fourth grade before I started entering these tests. But when I came out of these tests, finding out I entered a very good school [Üsküdar American], this was a very good competition, I even thought it was entertaining sometimes, but like Ulya said, if I did not win, it would be bad.

U: After a while, you start adjusting to the situation. For example, I thought sixty minutes studying was fifty minutes work and ten minutes break. Because I started to see this ten-minute break as a prize, studying became joyful. After a while working, really, I was not doing too much, uncomfortable. . . . I was not complaining, but I was enjoying it by saying, "finish geography, finish social, finish science," I started to enjoy it a lot.

Z: You sit down and talk about all this to the child. Ten days before the test, we stop the tutoring, very easy studying, we kept it for talking with Esra. We brainwashed her like a psychologist, so she would not be depressed; we thanked her for the work she had done.

F: You have to talk in a way that if there is a failure . . . this is a big possibility . . . they don't go in a depression, and feel guilty, and [this doesn't] affect their life. You have to give them the space without making them feel too comfortable. This is a very critical point. The child is preparing for the test while also being taught to accept failure. So they don't get affected from the result.

Z: I sat down and talked to Esra. I thanked her for sitting down and working with me for a year (instead of her thanking me), because she finished her responsibility. After this, if the result is positive or negative, whatever it is, that is not important for me, all the good things she learned during this, for all that I thanked her.

F: We haven't talked about Hatice. She is our psychologist and teaches at Istanbul University. She has known our children from when they were three months old. She really helped us. Even though we go every year, I decided to go every month during the fifth grade. For example, my daughter has a concentration problem. This exam takes one hour and a half to complete. Ulya has to concentrate for that period. She had Ulya start from twenty minutes and had her concentrate until she was able to concentrate for an hour and a half. There are many little things that actually need to be taken seriously, like the sitting position, the breathing method, how and where it will be better. . . . We learned all of these from Hatice.

Z: Hatice can tell from their eyes what they are doing. Also, she had me take Esra to a concentration specialist when she was in either fourth or fifth grade. She had trouble paying attention. We went to another psychologist. Esra worked with her for a while. Like you said earlier, the breathing technique helps a lot during panic and anxiety.

F: So it really helps the child psychologically. It really helps them get control of their anxiety. Both of the children went [to the school where the SMSEs was given] by themselves and were not excited at all.

In my opinion, that was their best advantage. They went and took the exam as if it were a normal part of their daily routine. The psychologist helped them realize that their life would not change negatively if the exam went badly. The psychologist really helped in this matter.

Money

Z: There is also a financial side to the SMSEs. The cost of all this preparation is terrible. You cannot really have a total figure, because the tutors are paid every minute. But, let's say last year, hourly TL 75 million [$75] was the starting price for the simplest tutor. But this depends on the tutor. There are ones for a TL 100 million [$100]—depends on your tutor. Imagine having this all the time. The figures are scary. You cannot have a net figure. Besides this, there are test books. Because tutors and parents are always together, there is a cost of hosting and serving too. That's costly too, everyday cake, tea, cake, tea, this is not a joke, this is seven days a week, not one day. This is very costly.

F: I am lucky on that matter. I was going to someone else's home. There are no hidden costs. And also because there are two children being tutored, it is less costly for me—I say this always, here and there, that we got it cheap. But of course we paid the tutor twice a week. But it was a group class, that's why it was not as costly. And also we went to someone else's house. Sometimes I ended up with being friends with the hosting parent, I could even stay for eating sometimes. I had a very economical experience.

A: I will answer it this way, minimum $20,000 in one year. If you consider starting this at the fourth grade, that means times two. For the tutor it is $20,000, plus the books, plus the commute expenses. I am guessing—you can also . . . if you also add a course to this, it can be $25,000. So if you add one more tutor and a course, it will be like $30,000 dollars at the end for the year.

Destinations

For new middle-class parents, the education mission underlying their determination to have their children succeed in the private SMSE was to place them in the best middle schools and to prepare them for the Turkish University Entrance Examinations (ÖSS). The university examinations were part of an overall strategy that began when their children were in primary school. Because only the top 10 percent of test-takers will enter the Turkish universities, parents tend to plan for a child's future very early. In contrast with the SMSEs, the university examinations can be repeated. The goal of new middle-class parents, however, was not only to win the right for their child to enter a university, but to win a place in one of the few top universities. The education issue that is most politically sensitive in Turkey is the crisis of higher education. The new private universities help to ameliorate the quality issue, but their small enrollments come nowhere near ameliorating the growing number of students who seek quality public university degrees. The first choice of many new middle-class families, of course, is to send their child to a foreign university.

Roll Call

There follows a list of a sample of parents who persevered through our inquiries as well as the all-important task of leading their young children through years of preparation to take the SMSEs. Our own understanding of success or failure rests on how well the outcome matches the expectations of parents. This relative assessment privileges parents' own views about their efforts, in contrast with society's views of them. The interviewees' names appear in bold print.

Metin Aklar (2006): He and his wife have three children. The two oldest children have taken the SMSEs. His fourteen-year-old daughter won the highest-rated public school, Istanbul Erkek Lisesi. She also won a place in Alman Lisesi, where Hasan and his wife decided to send her. His eleven-year-old daughter prepared for the SMSE during the month that we held the interview. She won the private SMSE and followed the path of her parents to Robert Lisesi.

Hasan and Nuran Uzun (2006): After Can's performance in the SMSEs, Hasan and Nuran decided to send Can to private Ataköy Kültür Koleji in Bakırköy. During those years, the school prepared Can well in English, fulfilling the parents' expectation of foreign language. Can entered the new Eighth Grade Exam and scored high enough to win a place in one of a small number of private science high schools. After he did well in his university examinations, he decided to study material science engineering. Now he is completing a university degree while working at the TUBITAK Marmara Research Center and looking ahead to graduate school, perhaps abroad. His parents, both university graduates, did not push him. They were delighted at their son's growing maturity and with his development.

Fatma Aslan (2006): Fatma and her husband Korkut, who is a medical doctor, wanted their daughter Ulya to win Robert Lisesi. Ulya was a quick learner in an elementary school, where she had a teacher who encouraged her parents to get involved in the test. Her year of preparation with a well-known tutor and a psychologist resulted in the highest score on the private SMSE. She entered Robert Lisesi. After graduation she was admitted to Dartmouth College, an Ivy League school in the United States. She graduated in 2003 and is now studying at Maryland Institute College of Art in Baltimore. Eventually she wants to open a gallery in Turkey.

Zuhal and Ata Yener (2006): When their daughter Esra entered the private SMSE preparation year, her aunt Fatma (see above) moved into the same apartment building to help Zuhal prepare Esra for the private SMSE. Fatma's experience and strategy paid off. Esra won a place in Üsküdar Amerikan Lisesi. After she graduated, she applied to and was admitted to private Hamilton College in the United States. After graduation, she returned to Istanbul to work in the media industry.

Ferda and Yavuz Bakan (2006): Ferda and Yavuz have a daughter Melek and a son Erkin. Melek studied psychology at York University in Toronto, Canada. After graduation, her parents encouraged her to work and stay in Canada, but she missed home and returned to Istanbul and recently became engaged. Erkin prepared for the private SMSE in 1996. Ferda had high expectations for him, but Yavuz was less concerned about winning one of the top private foreign-language schools. Erkin had difficulties during his preparation and his performance in the SMSE. He won a place in the Italyan (Italian) Lisesi, where he became interested in biology. Now he is in his second year at Pavia University in Italy.

Ayla and Kerim Taşkan (2006): They have a daughter Ece and a younger son. In the SMSE, Ece won both private Avusturya (Austrian) Lisesi and Galatasaray. Kerim chose the Austrian school because it teaches two languages and he also wanted her to learn Latin. He commented that "a graduate from an American school does not learn German, but a graduate from a German or Austrian school learns English." The Austrian government gives financial support to the student.

Sema Inan (2006): Sema has a daughter Burcu and a young son Ali. When Burcu's SMSE score was not high enough to win a place in a selective private school, Sema was able to put her on a waiting list at St. Benoit. But she was able to get Burcu into private Eyüboğlu Lisesi, where she remained through high school. After preparatory classes for the university examinations (ÖSS), she took them and was admitted to the Psychology Department at private Bilgi University in Istanbul. She has finished the first part of her second year.

A Final Note

Our intention has been to deconstruct the state's presumed rationality and its preoccupation with system logic by revealing the practices associated with educating the new middle class. The struggle between the state and family takes place in a context where parents must deal with a facticity created by the state that families recognize as "necessary," "very expensive," and "broken." Families are the victims of their own class consciousness when they are complicit in the state's determination to displace education with testing, learning with memorization, and deliberation with speed and accuracy. The irony is that the "quality" of education most desired by new middle-class families is delayed, and in some cases derailed, by years filled with endless tests that are the antithesis of the very education they desire. The irony is that the neoliberal era that has come to rely on tests, skill sets, and other techno-paraphernalia of education goes against the grain of the demand for individual creativity, innovation, and independence of thought that relies on new pedagogies, new ways to think, and an entrepreneurial spirit that is the antithesis of routinization, memorization, and an emphasis on speed and accuracy.

The education safety valve for Istanbul new middle-class families is neither in Turkey nor in Turkish private education, though the latter has recently made great strides toward meeting the demand for quality education. It is in other countries, through the attraction of foreign-language instruction and the experiences and social connections to be accumulated through living and learning abroad and bringing it all back that the symbolic capital of the new middle class is being accumulated and reproduced. From the larger perspective of globalization, the Istanbul new middle class is part of an emerging transnational middle class that serves the interests of a transnational capitalist class.

7

TESTING THE LIMITS OF
THE NEW MIDDLE CLASS

Istanbul new middle-class families could be excused for their obsession with testing. The state imposed a series of national tests that came to dominate the way in which families would think about themselves and their reproduction by means of education. First in order came the SMSEs for eleven-year olds that would determine who would take the small number of seats in the best middle schools. Then, in 1997, the SMSEs were replaced by the Eighth Grade Exam that would determine who would take the limited number of seats in the best high schools. The University Entrance Examinations followed soon after in the third year of high school. The demand for quality education continued to grow, outpacing every effort by the state or the private-school market to close the gap between demand and supply.

Education, in the sense of sending children to private or public elementary schools to learn the state curriculum, suffered from the pressures of competition. Schools came to be evaluated by test scores of their students. Teachers became known for their test methods, setting up a competition among teachers between and within schools. The public schools suffered teacher brain drains when they were attracted to private schools. The best teachers went from lower middle-class wages to being rich. As normal classroom education succumbed to testing, memorization and technique became more important in pedagogy. Learning became redefined and replaced by skills that increased speed and accuracy. The test encroached on daily classroom learning over an extended period. Many parents put their child in a school that offered half-day education as a tactic for saving time and money to buy more expert services.

Faced with unacceptable education alternatives, and combined with increasing pressure to develop a complete education strategy for each child, parents began surreptitiously comparing themselves with other families, creating a demand for expert services. Resistant to the very demand they were creating, parents noticed that other parents were finding a tutor for math or Turkish language or a particular subject. Before long, test results were rising, raising the bar for all. The search for better private schools added to their increasing cost. A market for tutors was created along with a market for lesson courses. The markets segmented into tutors for particular subjects, methods and lesson schools for particular subjects, and test information services. It was inevitable that the growing market for psychological services segmented along with the other markets to meet the needs of every mother and child that were specifically related to the anxiety, trauma, and depression associated with years of test preparation. Mothers became managers of children who became test machines. Fathers viewed themselves as money machines, complaining about the high costs of tutors, lesson schools, and private schools. The morbid expression for test preparation was "doping," a reference to adding hours of mindless memorization and endless past test questions to one's daily regimen.

From the founding of the republic, the drive to modernize was represented by engineers and symbolized by a discourse of engineering in ways that fetishized technology, math, and science. It remains so today. The engineering program in universities attracts those students who score highest on the university entrance examinations in math. Administrative "sciences" also attract high scores. Related fields such as architecture attract slightly lower scores. Those who enter with lower scores get in by selecting subjects in social sciences and humanities, reflecting the triumph of the neoliberal state over the welfare state. The most important subjects for winning the university entrance exams are math and Turkish. Social sciences, and especially humanities, are lower down in the university hierarchy, leading many parents to avoid these subjects if their child's score is high enough to enter one of the other departments.

The Rising Tide of Global Testing Raises All Tests

Istanbul new middle-class families can be excused for their obsession with testing because testing is a global trend that tracks the rise of neoliberalism as a hegemonic ideology for the purpose of rethinking education in global labor markets. In their interviews, Istanbul families allude to these problems of future employment. Turkey is among the original twenty-nine member states of the Organization for Economic Cooperation and Development (OECD), founded shortly after the end of World War II. The World Bank, founded in 1944, and the International Monetary Fund, founded in 1945, became key players in globalizing capital and creating the new economy. The rapid growth of gross domestic product (GDP) in the Turkish economy from 2001 to the present is due in part to the policies of those institutions. During the same period, there also was a significant increase in foreign direct investment (FDI).

The OECD promotes human capital analysis, the aim of which is to provide states and corporations with the economic tools to assess how best to spend their education budgets in ways that maximize the growth of human capital. Turkey's test system, while it deviates from some instruments and models of human capital accounting, bears a resemblance to its goals. For example, all those tests that families despise break education down into skill sets used to win the test. The outcome is a score in an objective set of scores. The scores become a form of human capital that, hypothetically, states and corporations can rely upon for investment in education.

Test scores also are embodied human capital that can be assessed directly in the labor market at the point of hiring. The European Personal Skills Card comes to mind (Spring 1998: 107–9). Investments in human capital are treated exactly like other capital investments in corporate human capital accounting. Through improving their skill sets, individuals increase their value in the market. This concept, referred to by human capital experts as "lifelong learning," within the logic and language of human capital investment, refers to an individual's continual need to upgrade his or her investment in oneself throughout the individual's life course. To the extent that the new economy relies on new technology of all kinds, education is a main arena of investment for the state, the corporation, and the worker. In human capital investment, all three march in step to the same tune, namely, "growing the economy" by means of further dispossession of state assets in every country. From the standpoint of the neoliberal persona, the self-worth of a worker undergoes continual transformation to stay in the work force. Under competitive pressure, continuous new waves of workers' human capital accumulation wash over existing workers human capital, ensuring obsolescence.

Investment in neoliberal education, for example, is indexed to objective measures of human capital. In the human capital perspective, the state or corporation is disinterested in how human capital is acquired. In the case of the Turkish test system, the state is a disinterested partner in how knowledge was acquired. It created subsystems in which education engineers manage and maintain the various parts of the machine: test design, preference and selection, administration of the test, and monitoring of outcomes. The whole system is a veneer of objective indicators of measured outcomes for every individual test-taker, measured and compared to others on a single scale, and used to evaluate the performance of each education institution. All agents of the system use the test outcomes as a measure of human capital development.

The introduction of Japanese national examinations is a case study that can be compared to the Turkish experience. In the 1960s, Japan created a modern system of schooling for economic development. The new language was "human resource management" (Spring 1998: 54). The idea was to sort students to meet human power needs. There were other considerations, such as the state's interest in having teachers follow the state curriculum and forcing them to teach to the test. "National testing was basic to using education for economic development" (1998: 54). Both goals are plausible in the case of Turkey. Spring states that, in the Japanese case, "The [OECD] language of the report captured the educational spirit of school systems serving the global economy" (1998: 55). The Japanese test is an efficient instrument for identifying talent early in life, planning for elite education, and sorting out future workers. The test ipso facto was a part of economic planning.[1]

The test was given at the end of compulsory education (junior high school) and was intended as an instrument to measure competencies and aptitudes as the bases of establishing paths to the future. Like Turkey's tests, the Japanese tests are demanding. The period of preparation is "*juken senso*," or "examination preparation war," reflecting its own culture history. In addition to regular school, there are private cram schools analogous to Turkey's lesson schools. There also are *jukus*, or privately operated neighborhood schools that give examination preparation on weekends or evenings. In contrast with Turkey's examination system, but in keeping with Japan's cultural history, there also are *yobiko* schools, full-day courses after the hours for school "for those who are masterless warriors who have failed the examinations" (Spring 1998: 56). A sizable number of students fit this category of future workers. Similar to Turkey, in the Japanese test system, the state uses education to manage national human capital development, in effect creating a class system for the cultural reproduction of material and social capital. Spring states that, "There is a direct relationship among family income, university attendance, and status of the university attended" (1998: 57). The analogy with Turkey is transparent. Ironically, Japan was the first country to experiment with neoliberal education after World War II and the first to abandon it. Japan recently has renounced its overheated emphasis on testing in favor of a system of pedagogy that relies on more innovative and exploratory education reforms.

We would be remiss if we were to end this book without highlighting a common theme that is woven into all the complexities we encountered in taped and informal interviews and the many conversations that we were privileged to participate in. New middle-class families' demand for private education has produced a range of alternative pedagogies. Education entrepreneurs like Lale Ünal are in high demand, but they run into a wall of state testing. In Istanbul, education is a positional good and parents must think straight about its value in the labor market. But they also believe strongly in the power of private education to make their children more aware of themselves, more involved in the world around them, and better persons. For Istanbul new middle-class parents, quality education is about making the person whole, living in a complex world that their children are eager to embrace, and providing them with the opportunity to explore the world through their five senses. Their understanding about the goals of quality education goes far beyond the narrow state and corporate goals of education.

Notes

1. For issues in education restructuring in the context of globalization and national policy, see Daun 2002. For comparative case studies, see especially Daun for "the richest countries" (chapter 4), Daun and Sapatoru for Eastern Europe (chapter 5), and Kanaev and Daun for Central Asia (chapter 8).

APPENDIX A
Istanbul Socioeconomic Household Survey, 1993

❖

This appendix describes a socioeconomic survey we conducted in the summer of 1993 that was used to identify some of the parameters that could be useful in locating an Istanbul new middle class. The survey questions cover a broad range of economic, social, and cultural indicators. We named the survey Global Integration of Turkey's Economy and Changing Household Consumption Trends (*Türkiye Ekonomisinin Global Entegrasyonu ve Değişen Hanehalkı Tüketim Eğilimleri*). The twenty-one-page survey, constructed by Balkan, consists of six parts and ninety questions. A condensed version in English is presented here.

The survey reflects our thinking at the time that we would study primarily consumer habits to understand the culture of the new middle class. In 1994, we shifted our research focus from lifestyle to education. The survey served its purpose in mapping socioeconomic characteristics of Istanbul new middle-class households in social space. Below are the main categories of the survey and some examples of questions that focused directly on our interest in exploring education, property, and some lifestyle characteristics of the new middle class.

The Survey Questionnaire

1). General Characteristics of Space and Location (7 questions)
    What district (*semt*) is this household (*hanehalki*) located in?
    What are the main reasons why you came to live in this district?
    When did you come to Istanbul?

2). Household Characteristics (18 questions)
    Household head is point of reference. Respondent chooses among one
       of several alternatives to each of the following questions:
    What type of residence is your apartment in?
    Do you own your apartment? If you rent, what type of arrangement do
       you have?

If you own your apartment, how did you pay for it? How many square
    meters is your apartment?
How many bedrooms? How many total rooms? How many bathrooms?
Do you have other homes than the one you are living in?

3). Individual Characteristics (16 questions)
    What is the household head's attained level of education?
    What is the household head's spouse's attained level of education?
    Does the household head know a foreign language? Which one(s)?
    Does the household head's spouse know a foreign language? Which
        one(s)?
    Do any other members of the household know a foreign language?
        Who? Which one(s)?
    Did the head of household graduate from high school? What was its
        name?
    Did the head of household's spouse graduate from high school? What
        was its name?
    Did the household head graduate from a university? Which one?
    Did the household head's spouse graduate from a university?
        Which one?
    If the household head works, what is her or his occupation?
    If the household head's spouse works, what is her or his occupation?
    How many members of this household work outside the home?
    Are there children in this household who attend school? What gender?
        What age?
    What type of school do they attend?

4). Food (21 questions)

5). Credit and Insurance (14 questions)
    Do you use a credit card(s)? Which one(s)? How long have you used a
        credit card?
    How frequently do you use your credit card?
    Do you have a credit card you can use outside Turkey?
    Do you own stocks?
    Do you possess gold, foreign currency, time deposits, real estate, other?

6). Vacation and Entertainment (14 questions)
    Do you have a summer home?
    Do you take a holiday in the summer? If so, how many days?
    Do you return to the same place every summer?
    Where did you go for your holidays this past summer?
    Did you travel outside of Turkey this past year? For what purpose?

Selecting Households

Given limited resources, our practical aim was to discover differences within
middle-class fragments that we could label *upper*, *core*, and *lower* middle-class

households. Our goal, constrained by money and labor, was to survey five hundred households in two months. The households we surveyed do not represent a systematic sampling of known parameters of the Istanbul population.

Many Istanbullus are suspicious of strangers in their neighborhood, apartment, or home. They also are reluctant to give personal information to strangers. We failed in our first strategy, which was to pick neighborhoods and buildings that would be occupied by people who fit our imagined characteristics. Our second strategy reflected our belief that class is a social phenomenon. Each of our eight assistants who administered the survey questionnaire, all of whom were Turkish university students (with a single exception), used family networks to find households that would allow us through the door and answer our questions. This approach succeeded more than we had imagined. A family member would call a relative, neighbor, or friend on the phone and ask the person to participate in the survey. Assistants used public transport to travel to all parts of the city, incurring costs in time and money, but with a result of high acceptances. Appointments were made in advance and people were prepared to assist and to take the time to give reliable answers to questions. By definition, our sampling relied on *social* connections among households. But we didn't know in advance whether these connections would be *class* connections. Only after a large number of interviews had been completed and a preliminary analysis was done did we discern the material, social, and cultural patterns of a new middle class in our data.

The Data

Households were assigned a code and survey questions were coded before raw data for each household were entered into a computer. Turkish student assistants in the Economics Department at Hamilton College then scrutinized the raw data set for errors in recording and entry. The results became the raw data set that was later recoded and sorted into other data sets for particular analyses. Microsoft Excel software was used to develop variables, code them, and do preliminary sorting and analysis. Turkish census codes were used to code our survey variables for districts, occupations, and other relevant variables. We later developed our own code for assigning households to social class by using a combination of education and occupation. Education was coded as a combination of attained level, school type, and presence or absence of foreign-language instruction. Occupation was coded by using a classification that distinguished professional/managerial categories from shopkeepers/clerks and skilled/unskilled labor categories.

Five hundred and fifty households were interviewed in the months of June and July 1993. The households were located in 102 districts widely distributed over the space of the whole city. Given the potential for high social diversity and wide differentiation in such a complex urban social structure, including differences between districts, our preliminary results were encouraging. Fifty-nine of the districts were assigned upper middle-class status and forty-three districts were assigned lower middle-class status "on inspection," i.e., based on our presuppositions. Of the 320 households in our survey that resided in the upper middle-class districts, only fifteen (4.7 percent) proved to be lower middle class in terms of survey data on occupation and education.

APPENDIX B

Interviews, 1996

The interviews were conducted in a variety of places and at different hours of the day, always at a place familiar to the person(s) being interviewed and at a time convenient to the interviewee(s). Most often, for parents, this meant at home after dinner in the evening, when those with employment outside the home would be present and parents could look after their children. These were the most hospitable settings, when the whole family greeted us at the door and everyone, including children, would sit in the salon in soft comfortable chairs, with soft lighting, and the interview would turn into an evening of conversation with hosts and guests over tea, coffee, and dessert. Visitors to a Turkish home receive very warm welcomes. Private tutors extended the same hospitality to our visits. On several occasions, we interviewed parents at their place of work. These were people who were busy or who valued the privacy of their home, but their reception was always hospitable and, once seated, they would take all the time necessary to explore our questions. In the case of school owners and administrators, we invariably met them at their schools in their private offices, where they were more than willing to talk about their own work histories, their businesses, and the relations and problems they had with departments in the Ministry of National Education. They talked about private education in Turkey today and offered their views on the examination system and how they prepared children and parents for the ordeal.

With a single exception, the interviews were recorded in Turkish and translated into English. Most were between sixty and ninety minutes in length. Interviews followed a schedule of questions, but they were conducted in such a way that people could take their own approach to the question or topic and explore it at length. If things went off track—this happened on occasion—the interviewer brought it back with the equivalent of "Well, what do you think of this?" Invariably the open-ended questions allowed for dialogical exploration of an issue or event rather than a direct answer.

For interviews with parents, we used the following list of questions to structure the interview:

1) How important is education in Turkish society today for ensuring a good future for your child?

2) What kind of future do you want for your child? What education would prepare your child for that future?

3) Have members of your family been involved in planning your child's education? In what ways? What things do you talk about together?

4) How did your family plan for your education? Was it different back then from the way it is now?

5) What is important to learn in school today? Why?

6) Do you worry about having enough resources to devote to your child's education?

7) What made you enter this race (the examination competition)?

8) What alternatives, if any, did you consider?

9) Do you think the examination system is fair? Has the Ministry of Education done the right thing in the circumstances of education in Turkey today?

10) How are you preparing your child for the examinations?

11) What schools are you considering for your preferences and why? What are your chances?

12) Have family members made personal sacrifices in the interest of the child's preparation?

13) We hope your child will win the race, but what will you do if she or he fails? Have you thought about this?

The tone of interviews is important to the interpretation of the meaning people give to their words, but the emotional content of a message is difficult to capture on the page. The topic of national examinations for eleven-year-olds is a provocative one. All parents we interviewed chose to enter their children in the examinations, but they did so under duress. The examinations are hated and yet the reality is that there is little alternative but to endure the long anxiety-producing process of preparation. Parents felt trapped by the state into having to put their children through the examination in a trade-off with lost childhood.

For interviews with various agents of private education and the examination industry, we followed the same procedure we did for parents. We constructed an interview schedule highlighting some of the following topics.

1) What is your educational background?

2) What is your present position?

3) What services do you provide?

4) In your opinion, do the SMSEs satisfy a need in Turkish education?

5) What are your relations with the Ministry of National Education?

BIBLIOGRAPHY

Anderson, Benedict. 1983. *Imagined Communities.* New York: Verso.

Balkan, E. and E. Yeldan. 1998. "Turkey." In *Financial Reform in Developing Countries*, eds. J. Fanelli and R. Medhora. New York: St. Martin's Press, Inc. 129–155.

Baloğlu, Zekai. 1990. *Türkiye'de Eğitim: Sorunlar ve Değişime Yapısal Uyum Önerileri.* Istanbul: TUSIAD Yayınları.

Baron, Stephen, John Field, and Tom Schuller, eds. 2001. *Social Capital: Critical Perspectives.* Oxford: Oxford University Press.

Boratav, K., O. Türel, and E. Yeldan. 1995. "The Turkish Economy in 1981–92: A Balance Sheet, Problems and Prospects." *METU Studies in Development* 22 (1): 1–36.

Bourdieu, Pierre. 1977. *Outline of a Theory of Practice.* Cambridge: Cambridge University Press.

———. 1991. *Language and Symbolic Power.* Cambridge, MA: Harvard University Press.

———. 1997. "The Forms of Capital." In Halsey, Lauder, Brown, and Wells 1997. 46–58.

Bourdieu, Pierre and Jean-Claude Passeron. 1990. *Reproduction in Education, Society, and Culture.* London: Sage Publications.

Brown, Phillip, and Hugh Lauder. 1997. "Education, Globalization, and Economic Development." In Halsey, Lauder, Brown, and Wells 1997. 172–192.

Carnoy, Martin. 2000. "Globalization and Education Reform." In Stromquist and Monkman 2000, 43–62.

Coleman, James S. 1988. "Social Capital in the Creation of Human Capital." *American Journal of Sociology Supplement: Organizations and Institutions: Sociological and Economic Approaches to the Analysis of Social Structure, Vol. 94*: 95–120.

Daneshklu, Sheherazade. 2007. "Emerging world's cities boast fastest rise in output." *Financial Times*, Wednesday, March 7.

Daun, Holgar, ed. 2002. *Educational Restructuring in the Context of Globalization and National Policy.* New York: RoutledgeFalmer.

———. 2002. "Education for Competitiveness and Diversity in the Richest Countries." In Daun 2002, 115–46.

Daun, Holgar and Dana Sapatoru. 2002. "Educational Reforms in Eastern Europe: Shifts, Innovations and Restoration." In Daun 2002, 147–180.

Davies, Bronwyn and Peter Bansel. 2007. "Neoliberalism and Education." *International Journal of Qualitative Studies in Education* 20 (3): 247–59.

Duben, Alan and Cem Behar. 1991. *Istanbul Households*. Cambridge: Cambridge University Press.

Ellul, Jacques. 1964. *The Technological Society*. New York: Alfred A. Knopf

Emiroğlu, Ibrahim. 1995. *Anadolu Liseleri*, Izmir: Cumhuriyet Matbaası.

Engels, Frederick. 1942. *The Origin of the Family*. New York: International Publishers Co., Inc.

Fortna, Benjamin C. 2002. *Imperial Classroom: Islam, the State, and Education in the Late Ottoman Empire*. New York: Oxford University Press.

Foucault, Michel. 1978. "On Governmentality." *Ideology and Consciousness* 6: 5–22.

———. 1994. "The Subject of Power." In *Michel Foucault: Power*, ed. J. Faubion. New York: New Press.

Frey, Frederick W. 1965. *The Turkish Political Elite*. Cambridge, MA: MIT Press.

Gellner, Ernest. 1983. *Nations and Nationalism*. Ithaca, NY: Cornell University Press.

Gramsci, Antonio. 1971. *The Prison Notebooks*, eds. Q. Hoare and G. Nowell Smith. New York: International Publishers.

Green, Andy. 1990. *Education and State Formation*. London: Macmillan.

Hallak, Jacque. 2000. "Globalization and Its Impact on Education." In Mebrahtu, Crossley, and Johnson 2000. 21–40.

Halsey, A. H., H. Lauder, P. Brown and A. S. Wells(eds.). 1997. *Education, Culture, Economy and Society*. New York: Oxford University Press.

Hanson, Allan F. 1993. *Testing, Testing*. Berkeley: University of California Press.

Harvey, David. 2003. *The New Imperialism*. Oxford: Oxford University Press.

———. 2005. A *Brief History of Neoliberalism*. Oxford: Oxford University Press.

Haydaroğlu, Polat. 1993. *Osmanlı Imparatorluğu'nda Yabancı Okullar*. Ankara: Ocak Yayınları.

Kanaev, Alexander and Holgar Daun. 2002. "Nationalism and Educational Transition in Central Asia." In Daun 2002, 227–44.

Kaplan, Samuel. 2006. *The Pedagogical State*. Stanford, CA: Stanford University Press.

Kasaba, Reşat, 1997. "Kemalist Certainties and Modern Ambiguities." In *Rethinking Modernity and National Identity in Turkey*, eds. Sibel Bozdoğan and Reşat Kasaba. Seattle: University of Washington Press. 15–36.

Kazamias, Andreas. 1965. *Education and the Quest for Modernity in Turkey*. Chicago: The University of Chicago Press.

Keyder, Çağlar. 1987. *State and Class in Turkey*. London: Verso.

———. 1999. "The Setting." In *Istanbul: Between the Global and the Local*, ed. Çağlar Keyder. 3–28. New York: Rowman and Littlefield.

Keyder, Çağlar and Ayşe Öncü. 1993. *Istanbul and the Concept of World Cities*. Istanbul: Friedrich Ebert Foundation.

Kocabaşoğlu, Dr. Uygur. 1989. *Anadolu'daki Amerika*. Istanbul: ARBA Yayin Tic.

Lomnitz, Lorrisa. 1971. "Reciprocity of Favors in the Urban Middle Class of Chile." In *Studies in Economic Anthropology*, ed. George Dalton. 93–106. Washington, DC: American Anthropological Association.

Lury, Celia. 1996. *Consumer Culture*. Cambridge: Polity Press.

Mebrahtu, Teame, Michael Crossley, and David Johnson, eds. 2000. *Globalization, Educational Transformation, and Societies in Transition*. Oxford: Symposium Books.

Moran, A. Vahid. 1999. *Büyük Türkçe-İngilizce Sözlük: A Turkish-English Dictionary*. Istanbul: Adam Yayınları.

Öncü, Ayşe. 1997. "The Myth of the 'Ideal Home' travels across Cultural Borders to Istanbul." In *Space, Culture, and Power: New Identities in Globalizing Cities*, ed. Ayşe Öncü and Petra Weyland. 56–72. London: Zed Books.

Perrucci, Robert and Earl Wysong. 1999. *The New Class Society*. New York: Rowman and Littlefield.

"Photo of Boy with His Father and Tutor." *Cumhuriyet*. 6 July 1995.

Picasso, Pablo. 1927–28. "The Studio." New York: Museum of Modern Art.

Polanyi, Karl. 1944. *The Great Transformation*. New York: Rinehart.

Polanyi, Karl, Conrad Erensberg, and Harry W. Pearson, eds. 1957. *Trade and Market in the Early Empire*. Glencoe, IL: The Free Press.

"Private School Champion from a State School." *Milliyet*, 16 June 1995.

"Public Schools Don't Measure Up to Private Schools." *Yeni Yüzyıl*, 22 May 1997.

Rodrik, Dani. 1991. "Premature Liberalization, Incomplete Stabilization: The Ozal Decade in Turkey." In *Lessons of Economic Stabilization and Its Aftermath*, eds. M. Bruno, S. Fisher, E. Helpman, N. Liviatan, and L. Meridor, 323–58. Cambridge, MA: MIT Press.

Sahlins, Marshall. 1965. "On the Sociology of Primitive Exchange." In *The Relevance of Models for Social Anthropology*, ed. Michael Banton. 139–206. London: Tavistock Publications.

Savage, Mike, James Barlow, Peter Dickens, and Tony Fielding. 1992. *Property, Bureaucracy and Culture*. New York: Routledge.

Schuller, Tom, Stephen Baron, and John Field. 2001. "Social Capital: A Review and Critique." In *Social Capital: Critical Perspectives*, eds. Stephen Baron, John Field, and Tom Schuller. Oxford: Oxford University Press.

Spring, Joel. 1998. *Education and the Rise of the Global Economy*. Mahwah, NJ: Lawrence Erlbaum Associates.

Shaw, Stanford, 1976–77. *History of the Ottoman Empire and Modern Turkey*. New York: Cambridge University Press.

Stromquist, Nelly P. and Karen Monkman, eds. 2000. *Globalization and Education: Integration and Contestation across Cultures*. New York: Rowman and Littlefield.

Sumner-Boyd, Hilary and John Freely. 1989. *Strolling Through Istanbul*. Istanbul: Redhouse Press.

"Super Twins of Examination." *Milliyet*, 31 May 1995.

"They Rely on Their Teachers." *Yeni Yuzyil*, 23 May 1997.

Thompson, E. P. 1963. *The Making of the English Working Class*. London: Golancz Ltd.

Thompson, John B. 1991. "Editor's Introduction." In *Language and Symbolic Power*, Pierre Bourdieu, Cambridge, Mass. Harvard University Press. 1–31.

Toprak, Binnaz. 1995. "Civil Society in Turkey." In *Civil Society in the Middle East*, Volume Two, ed. Augustus Richard Norton. Leiden: E.J. Brill. 87–118.

Vahapoğlu, Hidayet. 1992. *Osmanlıdan Günümüze Azınlık ve Yabancı Okulları*. Istanbul: Boğaziçi Yayınları.

Wacquant, Loic, J.D. 1991. "Making Class: The Middle Classes in Social Theory and Social Structure." In *Bringing Class Back In*, eds. Scott G. McNall, Rick Fantasia, and Rhonda F. Levine. 39–63. Boulder, CO: Westview Press.

Williams, Raymond. 1973. *The Country and the City*. New York: Oxford University Press.

Wolf, Eric. 1981. *Europe and the People without History*. Berkeley: University of California Press.

Wright, Erik Olin. 1989. *The Debate on Classes*. New York: Verso.

The New Turkish Investment Environment. 2006 Istanbul: YASED International Investors Association.

Yeldan, E. 1995. "Surplus Creation and Extraction Under Structural Adjustment: Turkey, 1980–1992." *Review Of Radical Political Economics* 27 (2): 38–72.

Zaim, Osman. 1995. "The Effects of Financial Liberamlization on the Efficiency of Turkish Commercial Banks." *Applied Financial Economics* 5: 257–64.

INDEX